WHAT AMERICA MEANS TO ME

Albert F. Chestone
(Retired FBI Agent)

First published by Dog Ear Publishing
4010 W. 86th Street, Ste H
Indianapolis, IN 46268
www.dogearpublishing.net

ISBN: 978-159858-895-8

This book is printed on acid-free paper.
This book is non-fiction. Unless otherwise noted, the author and the publisher make no explicit guarantees as to the accuracy of the information contained in this book and in some cases the identity of some authors of articles set forth herein have been reported as unknown.

Printed in the United States of America

TABLE OF CONTENTS

Foreword.........Simon Ruebens   vii

Acknowledgements   xiii

Introduction.........Albert F. Chestone   xv

The Constitution of a Citizen

Chapter One   I Believe......... John D. Rockefeller, Jr.   3
Chapter Two   Oath of Allegiance.........William Tyler Page   5
Chapter Three   What Is An American?.........Peter Ferrara   7
Chapter Four   What Does it Mean to Be an American
                       Citizen?.........The Hon. Lee H. Hamilton   10

Land That I Love

Chapter Five   The America I Love.........Elie Wiesel   19
Chapter Six   What's So Great About America.........
                       Dinesh D'Souza   23
Chapter Seven   The Americans.........Gordon Sinclair   32
Chapter Eight   Ode To America.........Cornel Nistorescu   35

In God We Trust

Chapter Nine   Enough is Enough.........Rick Scarborough   39
Chapter Ten   The Lost Purpose of History.........
                       Hilmar von Campe   43
Chapter Eleven   Americanism vs. Islamism: A Personal
                       Perspective, 12th Annual Templeton
                       Lecture on Religion and World Affairs.........
                       Zuhdi Jasser   46

A Patriot's Glance At American History

Chapter Twelve   President Reagan's Farewell Address
                      to the Nation.........Ronald Reagan   52
ChapterThirteen   The Great Christmas Night Raid.........
                      W. Thomas Smith, Jr.   56
Chapter Fourteen   A Patriot's History of the United States.........
                      Dr. Larry E. Schweikart   61
Chapter Fifteen   Cheers and Tears.........Lt. General C.G. Cooper   62
Chapter Sixteen   A Memorial Day Message.........
                      Dr. James C. Dobson   69
Chapter Seventeen   The Flag of the United States of
                      America.........Howard Schnauber   79

All Men Are Created Equal

Chapter Eighteen   Martin Luther King's Conservative
                       Legacy.........Carolyn Garris   82
Chapter Nineteen   "I Have a Dream".........Martin Luther King, Jr.   85
Chapter Twenty   Remember 9/11.........Dr. Herbert I. London   90
Chapter Twenty-One   In Loving Memory of the Victims of the Terrorist
                      Attacks on Sept. 11, 2001.........Albert F. Chestone   93
Chapter Twenty-Two   Character – Courage – Community.........
                      Vincent J. Bove, CPP   95

A Nation of Immigrants

ChapterTwenty-Three   Addressing Illegal Immigration.........Robert Cox   100
Chapter Twenty-Four   Our Rich Treasure…Our Immigrants.........
                      Albert F. Chestone   102
Chapter Twenty-Five   A Letter from the Chairman.........
                      Mauro E. Mujica   107
Chapter Twenty-Six   English: Our Greatest Unifier.........Rob Toonkel   109

The Challenges of Freedom

Chapter Twenty-Seven   Why the Pledge of Allegiance Matters.........
                       Senator Tom McClintock   113
Chapter Twenty-Eight   America: Making Real the Promise of Hope.........
                       Dr. Paula A. Franzese   115
Chapter Twenty-Nine   The Meaning – and Demeaning – of
                       Patriotism.........Dr. Herbert I. London   118
Chapter Thirty   Bring Civics Lessons Back to the Classroom.........
                       Dr. Paula A. Franzese   125
Chapter Thirty-One   The Nature of Freedom.........Hilmar von Campe 128

America the Beautiful

Chapter Thirty-Two   History? Why? ....Joy Hakim   134
Chapter Thirty-Three   Land That I Love......... James F. McGuire   138
Chapter Thirty-Four   Personal Patriotic Expressions   140
Chapter Thirty-Five   The Rebirth of Patriotism.........
                       Albert F. Chestone   195
Chapter Thirty-Six   Patriotism Is Our Source of Strength.........
                       Albert F. Chestone   200

Foreword

America is a nation of awe-inspiring beauty.

The images come quickly to mind, from snowcapped mountains and majestic canyons to rolling hills and fields of wheat stretching far beyond the horizon. Yet, for me, America's greatest inspiration comes not from the wealth of its land but from the prize of its people—a flag of red, white, and blue that billows proudly as a symbol of our nation. Our flag bows to no one and, because of that, neither do I.

So what does America mean to me?

My answer is as multifaceted as America's people. But there is one recurring theme that resonates through everything that Americans are and everything that America is and can be—and that's freedom.

Each of us has the freedom to think, speak, and worship as we choose. Each of us can live and work as we see fit. Best of all, each of us has been blessed with the ability to influence change—not through force or intimidation, but through the freedom to become what we want, work hard, and vote our conscience. In America, dreams grow from the inside out. Like a mother's arms lovingly extended to her infant, it is our dreams that encourage us to take those tentative first steps toward the exciting possibilities that can only come with freedom.

Sometimes, I think we might forget that it's not like this everywhere. Of the many tragedies that can afflict us all, perhaps none is as devastating as the enslavement of the human spirit. In many countries, an oppressive past means nothing more than an oppressive future.

Maybe that's why so many people are willing to risk their lives to taste the freedom of America. Those who attempt to cross rough seas without a life-jacket or a desert without food and water consider such acts to be a badge of courage proudly worn—one that tells the world just how badly they cherish the freedom to make something of their lives.

While I have profound respect for such determination, I cannot fully understand its depth. As Aleksandr Solzhenitsyn once asked, "Can a man who is warm understand a man who is cold?" Probably not—especially for any man who has never felt the sting of a bitter wind. That's why, as blessed as I am, it may be unfortunate that since my birth I have only known freedom's comforting embrace.

My freedom has come at no personal cost. Strangely, I've never been asked to risk my life for freedom or even contribute a few years of service on its behalf. In the fall of 1969, my student deferment from active military service kept me far removed from the jungles of southeast Asia. As a college freshman, I could drink a beer and nuzzle a co-ed while my friends drafted directly from high school were being ambushed in fire fights far away.

I thought that was grossly unfair. But neither did I volunteer to serve. With vast freedoms, I had chosen to become slack if not irresponsible, and the insulation provided by two great oceans kept me focused inwardly on my own wants and needs. I accepted much too young that our freedom has so infrequently asked for anything in return. But the lesson I've come to learn is that freedom should never have to ask.

That hard truth made itself quite evident on September 11, 2001. On that morning, I traveled by train from my home in Connecticut to attend a business meeting in midtown Manhattan. It was a beautiful day with clear skies and a brilliant sun. As the train chugged across a railroad bridge from the Bronx, I could look down the East River and see towers of steel and glass gleaming in the distance.

A few hours later, Manhattan's two front teeth had been knocked out, leaving a gaping hole filled only by shock and disbelief. Later that afternoon, I began to walk toward Grand Central hoping to catch a train back home. I was numb. Suddenly, however, I could feel the hairs stand on the back of my neck.

Walking down Broadway, I came upon a deserted Times Square. It was three o'clock in the afternoon. No one was there. Suddenly, I asked myself if it were safe to be walking alone through an American icon that could be a prime target for terrorism. It was in that instant that I finally understood the great risks that will be taken by any man, woman, or child who is cold—because, on that day, someone tried to steal the warmth of freedom that is so fundamental to the nature of our nation.

Writing this foreword, therefore, is the very least that I can do in return for what America means to me. I am privileged that my father-in-law, a man from the greatest generation, asked me—a man from the generation that questioned everything—to make a contribution to his book.

With the news of Pearl Harbor, Al Chestone immediately left his freshman year at Ohio University to enlist in the Army Air Force, no questions asked. He was not alone. In Philadelphia, my father, Martin Ruebens, dropped out of high school midway through his sophomore year, lied about his age, and enlisted in the Navy. They heeded freedom's call. They were not alone. Countless men and women suspended their lives or gave them freely to fight for a cause greater than themselves.

Thanks to them and those who continue their example today far from our shores, I am able to exercise my freedom. Thanks to them, I am free to reformulate on a daily basis what America means to me. Whatever shading that America may take on for me on any particular day, however, is rooted in gratitude. Generations of brave Americans have given me a precious gift. What America means to me is the gift of freedom that is as life-sustaining as the air that I breathe.

In this book, you'll find what America means to many other people who took the time to share their feelings with my father-in-law. Al Chestone's book is a tapestry that illustrates the rich texture of the American experience. In reading his book, I am moved by the love of country that is held by so many today.

I am equally moved by the love of country that is felt just as deeply by those who will follow us tomorrow—from the young people who have enlisted in our armed forces to the young people who are enlisting others to register and vote for the very first time. Yet one of the most poignant examples of what America means to the youth of our country took place two seasons ago at an NFL football game in Charlotte, North Carolina.

Thanks to the Carolina Panthers and the Make-A-Wish Foundation, four young people diagnosed with an array of debilitating conditions had been granted a very special request. From the many things that they could have asked for, their wish was to stand at mid-field before more than 70,000 people and sing our National Anthem.

Ranging in age from 7 to 16 years, the quartet had practiced hard. When their moment came just before kickoff, they wanted to make sure that they knew the words. Said one of the singers, "We're going to rock this crowd."

They did—and, as you might imagine, their wish come true was celebrated with a thunderous standing ovation.

My wish for you is to read this book and to pause for just a moment to consider what America means to you. For me, it was a time to think—and to thank. Because when that anthem plays and those broad stripes and bright stars billow majestically in the breeze, I know it's a precious moment made possible only by the selfless sacrifice of people whose names I will never know.

Like this book, I honor them and the freedom they have bestowed upon me.

God bless our heroes.

And God bless the United States of America.

Simon Ruebens
Charlotte, North Carolina
February 18, 2009

I dedicate this book to:

All of my beloved family members my deceased wife Marcie, my children, grandchildren, stepchildren, step-grandchildren, brothers, sisters, parents, nieces, nephews and in-laws—both living and in heaven. Also to my beautiful and patient wife, Lorraine, who served as my guiding light as well as a constant source of encouragement for writing this book.

Acknowledgements

I am sincerely grateful to the wonderful, loyal and patriotic Americans who personally granted me permission to include some of their beautifully written works in this book.

I am indebted to Ms. Lynne Focaccia for her outstanding typing and organizational skills in the preparation of my manuscript. She is an exceptionally talented individual full of caring and kindness.

A special thank you to authoress Catherine Coulter for her kindness, assistance and guidance in the preparation of this book.

To Leslie Anderson, Publishing Manager, AuthorHouse for her thoughtful and kind assistance in the early stages of preparing this book.

Thanks to John Aramian, Executive Director of Red Sand Foundation, for his encouragement, wisdom and unfailing support. John is the creator of the Water Conservation Project, which set forth assignments for students in grammar school through college, known as "The Water Detectives" program. E-Mail: john@waterdetectives.org.

A special debt of gratitude to both Matthew Murry and Amber Ortner of Dog Ear Publishing, for their professional assistance toward the preparation of this book.

To my granddaughter, Lindsay Ruebens—without your editorial expertise, this project would not have been possible. There is a certain contagiousness about your enthusiasm.

Introduction

What America Means to Me
by Albert F. Chestone

I was moved to write this book based on my belief that if we are to remain a free, strong democracy as one nation under God, we must, with genuine and sincere faith, pledge allegiance to America.

We must stand united, determined to identify and expose the anti-Americans within our country, who have disregard for the labors of our Founding Fathers. The enemy exists within our society as both individuals and as well-funded organizations, chipping away at our Declaration of Independence and Constitution with a fierce determination to change our form of government. They are intent on eliminating any reference to God, knowing that the majority of our citizens are of the Judeo/Christian belief. We are Christians and Jews – and people of every faith, who believe in God – must stand tall, strong and vocal, against these enemies whose purpose is to deny us our full freedom. We must stand united and make certain that our lawmakers do not succumb to the demands of the enemy within and their rabble-rousing methods aimed at the destruction of our heritage, our culture, our form of government. If for no other reason, this then is "What America Means To Me."

America: My Birthplace, My Honor

I feel so privileged and honored to have been born in America. Like all Americans, I am a descendant of a foreign country. My parents were born in separate small villages in Italy and met each other years after their arrival in America in the late 1800s. Following a strict and formal engagement period, they married and settled in Waterbury, Connecticut, a city that was once known as "the brass center of the world."

During my childhood, life was difficult and suffering was evident in many forms. There was an excessively high rate of unemployment. Illness was common. People were hurt by discrimination and confronted with the barrier of what was for many a new and strange language – English. This was not only true of immigrants from Italy, but for virtually all immigrants intent on creating a new life for themselves and their families in America.

Yet, these brave immigrants gladly confronted their problems and struggled to make the most of their new lives without complaining about their sufferings and their setbacks. They were grateful for the privilege of being part of a free country and permitted to practice whatever religion they so desired. Obviously, this new land had a language of its own, so my parents much like all immigrants took pride in wanting to learn the English language and they did so, most willingly.

My mom was a beautiful woman, somewhat shy, but a wonderful story-teller, who held small groups of women spellbound by her stories. My dad was a kind and gentle person, who learned English by attending what was then called "night" school. He was determined to learn the trades of a toolmaker and tool-setter, and he did. For many years, he proudly practiced his trade with the Scovill Manufacturing Company in my hometown of Waterbury.

During the 1920s and early 1930s, America suffered a crippling depression. Most high school graduates had no choice but to forego a college education and work to support their families. My family endured the Great Depression years. It was humbling to stand in welfare lines for food and clothing. Social standing did not matter, nor did the talents one possessed. You could be a gifted musician, a sensational athlete, an expert in your trade – it didn't matter. Everyone had to stand in line to get a nub of bread and a tin of thin, steaming soup. Everyone had to stand in line to accept the well-worn but clean clothing of others. Everyone had to cope. It was a tough time.

Those who lived during the years of the Great Depression know full well the meaning of human suffering and humility. I was a child but completely aware of the sadness and sufferings of countless American families of all ethnic backgrounds, brought about by this horrific Depression. Yet we managed to withstand the pain and pulled together. As most families did, we always managed to draw closer together at dinner time. Either my mom or dad would give a blessing. No one was permitted to leave the table until everyone had eaten whatever it was we had that night. Whatever it was, we were grateful for it.

More often than not, immediately after dinner my dad would gather all the shoes that needed repair and proceed to his special space in the basement. Perhaps it was there that he was most at home. He would adjust the anvil on his lap, take hold of his hammer and nails, and resole our shoes with scrap pieces of leather.

Were we poor? Of course. But so were my very dear and close Irish, French, Polish, German, Scandinavian, Asian, South American, Mexican and African American buddies. Yet, we were able to laugh and play simple games without venting anger or spilling hatred because of our circumstances.

Our biggest thrill was to hold a small American flag and run with it so that it would flap in the breeze. We were a mixture of many nationalities and races but to all of us, our flag was the only symbol we needed to make us so proud to know that we were Americans.

I was so fortunate to have been raised in an area where all of us were the same – poor. I still treasure the years spent growing up with some remarkable down-to-earth individuals. I remember them well. Sadly, most of them have passed away.

During my grammar school days, I recall helping my brother Henry on Saturdays at an A&P store where he enjoyed his title of "main delivery boy." Every week, Henry pulled down $2.50, plus the Saturday night take-home of all the stale bread and leftover goodies he could stuff into his coat and pockets. When I entered high school I managed, with my mother's help, to obtain a job as a delivery boy in a meat market on Saturday mornings where I earned a dollar in exchange for four hours of my time.

I have fond memories of my education. I learned the basics from some wonderful teachers at Wilby High School, and had the greatest friends in the world. Like me, many of them played sports. I played baseball (pitcher less than fair) and basketball for four years, but I didn't excel enough to qualify for any type of athletic scholarships.

However, based on my interest in school work and sports, I became motivated to further my education rather than settle for learning a factory trade. I decided to work for one year after graduation and did so with a promise to myself that I would turn over my weekly earnings to my mother. She kept my dimes and quarters in a shoebox – not for herself or for her family, but so that I could be the first – and, as the youngest of six – only member of my family who would go to college.

What is the point of telling you all of this?

America was different then. It was the early 1940s. So many were poor. Yet, for some reason, all of us had high hopes that this wonderful land of great freedoms would also prove to be a wonderful land of great opportunities.

For me, opportunity came calling one day during a visit from Reverend Father Dial, who asked if I would help introduce basketball at Sacred Heart High School for the first incoming class of boys in what was previously an all-girls school. I gladly accepted this non-paying position. At the age of 18, I was one of the youngest high school basketball coaches in New England.

While we did not break any records, we won a few and lost a few more, but it was a rewarding experience. It gave me an opportunity to witness the determination and dedication of young athletes with big hearts. Since then, Sacred Heart High School basketball teams have broken records and have developed into a powerhouse team. It has been very satisfying to see this team grow and develop from the team I helped guide at its very beginning.

From a Campus to a Military Base

In the Fall of 1941, I left for college with two of my friends, Bill Carroll and Bob Shumway. Our destination was Ohio University in Athens, Ohio, a bumpy 18-hour drive from Waterbury in Bill's model T-Ford.

Bill and I became roommates. Mindful of my total college savings of $850, I immediately asked the landlady if I could do some housework to pay for my room. She said that if I would make eight beds every morning, I would not have to pay boarding costs. I accepted without hesitation.

That took care of my room. But I also had to find a way to eat. Fortunately, I met another freshman who told me that he worked as a dishwasher in the kitchen at a girl's dormitory where he was able to get three meals a day. I asked him immediately if there were any other openings. He took me under his wing and managed to get me to assist him as a dishwasher. I was now able to eat three meals a day. I shall always be indebted to my good friend, Tony DiBiasio, now deceased, and a legend in Lakewood, Ohio.

On Sunday morning, December 7, 1941, I was walking across campus with some friends to go play touch football, when I heard my friend Bill McCutcheon (who after graduation became a TV star and Broadway actor, now deceased) call out to me from a fraternity house, "Chesty, we're at war! Pearl Harbor was just bombed!"

All of us were shocked and stunned, wondering what to do. Many of us enlisted in various branches of the service. I chose the Air Force.

Eventually, I found myself in uniform at Ft. Devens, Massachusetts. Shortly thereafter, I shipped off to McDill Field and Drew Field in Florida, then off to Fargo, North Dakota, and to a final stop in Biloxi, Mississippi, where I somehow pulled KP for many days.

While serving eggs one morning to a visiting Army Physical Instructor, I accidentally made the mistake of not giving him enough. He yelled for a larger portion and I was about to follow his order, but as I glanced at him, and he stared at me, we both broke into broad smiles, warmly shook hands and embraced. This Physical Instructor was the kind football player who helped me obtain a dishwasher's job at Ohio U, my friend, Tony DiBiasio. It was truly an unexpected reunion.

It was not long after this experience that I found myself together with a new buddy, Archie Andersen from Fargo, North Dakota, on a Liberty ship, one of many leaving the Patrick Henry Harbor at Norfolk, Virginia, for a destination unknown to us at the time. After a few days at sea, we encountered high winds and frightening waves both of which caused many of us to develop stomach problems.

The huge convoy of Liberty ships was a sight to behold. We exchanged hand greetings daily to the men on nearby ships and did many things to keep ourselves occupied as we kept wondering where we were headed. After almost a month at sea, it appeared that part of the convoy continued North, apparently toward England, while our group of ships proceeded through the Straits of Gibraltar and eventually docked in the Port of Oran, Africa. The war was still being waged in North Africa where the brave Australians and British troops were defeating the German Army.

Within several days after victory in North Africa, we boarded our particular Liberty ship and set sail across the Mediterranean Sea. We were told that we were being followed by a German U-Boat, obviously wanting to know where we were headed. A day or so later we heard loud blasting sounds. The U-Boat would no longer be following us.

It was quite dark when we arrived near the port of Bari, Italy. A number of sunken ships, their masts jutting out of the water, made it difficult for our Liberty ship to pull into port. The captain of our ship, however, arranged for a native Italian ship navigator to come aboard. He managed to maneuver the ship through the narrow passageways that allowed the ship to be safely anchored.

In the quiet of the night, we left the ship and climbed aboard waiting army trucks. We traveled for what seemed like an eternity through winding streets and eventually found our way to an old school house that would serve as an operational center for our Armament Division of the 55th Bomb Wing of the 15th Air Force, located in Spinnazola, Italy. Our unit was responsible for arming the fleet of B-24 bombers with the proper bombs for their particular missions. Within a short time, our unit was totally organized and ready to service the needs of our four bomb groups, which we did quite satisfactorily and with great pride.

An Unexpected Surprise

During the early stages of organizing our various units, it became necessary for all of us to stand guard in this new strange town over our motor pool vehicles. Guard duty was a necessity for many reasons. For one, the leather seats of our vehicles were an attractive item in North Africa, especially for footwear. We felt that the townspeople might have the same attraction.

It so happened that on one of my tours of guard duty, a cute little girl, about three or four years old, was standing across the street. I waved to her in a friendly manner. She smiled and waved back to me. In my broken Italian language, I asked her to tell me her name. She responded, "Ninetta." I asked her if she liked chocolate and she responded, "si," yes. I told her that I would have some for her the next day because I would be back on duty again. She nodded. I knew she would be back.

On the following day I reported to the same post. Within minutes my new little friend appeared at the top of an embankment. I waved to her. As I began to reach in my pockets for some chocolate bars, I noticed that she was inviting others to the party. Sure enough, Ninetta had invited four older girls to come along. They were her sisters. They ranged in ages from about 3 to 17. Fortunately, I had more than enough bars to share with them. They crossed the street to my post to express their thanks and shyly shared their names: Ninetta, Teresa, Gigina, Carmela and Maria.

Every time thereafter, whenever I was assigned to that same post, I managed to see and wave to these five beautiful sisters and utter some mispronounced Italian words that would cause them to laugh. Their laughter gave me joy. As I came to know them, I could not help but notice they needed food and clothing. Their parents were only able to do so much.

Reunited Love

One day I learned that the eldest girl, Maria, had met and fallen in love with an American soldier from Tennessee, Roy West. He had spent time in this village as an army engineer, but his unit had to move on to a new northern location. This of course caused Maria such heartache knowing that Roy could be wounded or killed by the retreating German army. I felt confident that he would survive, so as the war began to wind down, I felt the urge to prepare the family for this special homecoming, not knowing for certain when he would be returning to Spinnazola.

I took it upon myself to request my family and friends back home in Waterbury to send me packages of clothing for girls ranging in ages from 3 to 17. At every opportunity, I delivered these packages to my new found, unofficially adopted girls and, of course, they were thrilled. By the time the war had finally ended, I had developed a very close friendship with the entire family. In doing so, my ability to speak Italian improved.

Immediately following the end of the war, our wish came true. Maria's American boyfriend, Roy West, returned and within a day or two, plans were made for a wedding to be held in a small Catholic church in Spinnazola. I was presented with the honor of not only being the best man for Roy, but was asked to Americanize the wedding ceremony, which I did to the best of my knowledge. The wedding took place most joyfully and an entertaining reception followed with much song and laughter. There were tears of joy that Maria and Roy had married, but also tears of sorrow in knowing that this lovely angel, Maria of Spinnazola, Italy, would soon be leaving her beautiful village to live in Tennessee.

An Unexpected Departure

A few days after the wedding of the new Mr. and Mrs. Roy West, I received military orders to leave Italy and report to an airbase in the United States, where I was to be indoctrinated on matters relating to armaments for the B-29 bombers being used in the war against Japan.

Somehow some of the villagers and the young sisters had learned of my departure orders. This was not what I had wished. I knew that for me this departure would be very emotional. It so happened that on the early morning of my arranged departure, I exited the school headquarters building to board a waiting military vehicle, and was greeted by my many villager friends and, of course, the little sisters and their parents. They were sobbing and, soon, I was too. I completely caved in to the emotional exchanges of warm embraces. Somehow, I managed to climb aboard the military truck from which I waved and threw kisses, not knowing when our paths would cross again, if ever.

Homecoming

Strangely enough, shortly after my arrival at my new base in the United States, the Japanese surrendered. The war in the Pacific theater was over. All training plans were cancelled and new plans were quickly put into place for accelerating the orderly discharge of soldiers to a normal civilian life.

Like thousands upon thousands of soldiers, I waited anxiously to be informed of any discharge. The thrill and joy of returning home for every GI was beyond description. I, together with my two soldier brothers arrived home within days of each other. We were so lovingly embraced by all members of our family. Tears warmly trickled down our faces as my mother ran her hands across our arms and legs to be assured that they were actually our own.

This was a homecoming I shall never forget. For a long time afterward, however, I could not help then, as I still cannot help now, from time to time think about all the courageous young 19, 20, 21-year old kids who were killed while defending our country. They would never be able to experience the warm embraces of family members. I can't help but think about all the brave soldiers, who fought for all of us, all of them who lost their sight, their arms, their legs, or their lives. Their sacrifices for us came at a high price, which have truly added to the significance of "What America Means To Me."

Return to Campus

In the Fall of 1946, I returned to Ohio University where I was reunited with my fraternity brothers of Phi Delta Theta. Something was quite obvious. The college boys who had left a few years earlier came back as men.

My new roommate was Bob McKellogg, a native of Ohio and one of the finest individuals I have ever met. Since we were both returning war veterans, we made a pledge to truly apply ourselves to our studies and to do the best we could. We did. The war gave us a new sense of perspective. We returned with a sense of purpose. It seemed that aside from our involvement with our fraternity, we spent much time studying rather than going out on dates. That wasn't hard for Bob. He had a steady lady-friend, Clare Fitzgerald, who was attending a girl's college in Pennsylvania. Eventually they married and settled down in Fullerton, California, where they raised a large family. Unfortunately, Bob was called to heaven several years ago.

Little did I know that an important turning point in my life was about to begin. I remember the day very clearly. On January 11, 1947, I noticed an attractive young lady in the library. She was checking out several books from the library clerk. I had noticed her name, "Marcie," on a slip of paper that extended out from one of her books.

There was an aura about her that immediately told me she was special. She gathered her books from the library clerk, turned, and walked away. I was disappointed. While I had fought in a war, I did not have the courage to introduce myself to this beautiful young woman. Watching her walk away, I knew that it would be unlikely that I would ever meet up with her again.

When I returned to my fraternity house, I mentioned my library experience with the girl named Marcie to one of my fraternity brothers, Rudy Calabria. What happened next changed my life. Rudy asked me to repeat her name. I did. He said that his campus girlfriend had a new roommate whose name he believed was Marcie. Rudy called his girlfriend to ask about her new roommate. When his girlfriend said that her name was Marcie, Rudy asked if Marcie had been at the library just a short time earlier. She had. Rudy arranged for all of us to go out to the movies on a double date the very next day. This campus relationship continued after my graduation into the Fall Semester of 1947, when there was another major turning point in my life. I received a telegram from the Director of the FBI, J. Edgar Hoover, informing me that I had been accepted for training as a Special Agent of the FBI. If I wished to accept the invitation, I should respond without delay and report for duty at FBI Headquarters in Washington, D.C. The starting yearly salary would be $4,500. On February 2, 1948, I reported as instructed.

My New Profession

The first two young men I met upon my early arrival at the Bureau Headquarters were Jack Tuttle of the Bay Ridge section of Brooklyn, New York, and Jack Temple from Los Angeles brother of Shirley Temple. We remained close friends throughout our Bureau career.

My first assignment took me to Butte, Montana. I was thrilled to interview cowboys and Indians – real cowboys who rode the range and Native Americans of various tribes. I handled a variety of cases in Montana and at times I covered special investigations in Idaho.

After handling some rather interesting and delicate cases during a brief assignment in San Francisco, I was eventually transferred to New York. I made the move with mixed emotions, only because I had just begun to get acclimated to life in San Francisco and wondered if I could handle the fast-paced life of New York City.

In just a matter of time, however, I realized how fortunate I was to work in such a great city – and had another turning point in my life. On June 25, 1949, I married Marcelyn (Marcie) Scatterday, the pretty girl I had not had the courage to introduce myself to in the library at Ohio University. That was some blind date that my friend Rudy Calabria had arranged.

Marcie and I moved into an apartment in Stuyvesant Town in New York. Our monthly rent was the grand sum of $102.00. During the five years we lived in Stuyvesant Town, we had three children, Lynn, Sue and Tom. Somehow I managed to take night and weekend courses at New York University and obtain my Master's Degree. My life had changed forever and for the good. America had given me many opportunities and I was grateful for them.

As a new agent in the New York FBI Office, I was initially assigned cases that required background investigations on individuals seeking employment with the federal government. Such investigations required interviews with references. I met some fascinating people along the way – Edward R. Murrow and Frank Stanton at CBS; actor Charles Laughton and Mrs. Douglas MacArthur. Each of them were gracious and extremely cooperative. It was an exciting introduction to what would become a career of handling matters related to counter-intelligence for approximately 25 years.

In the Spring of 1954 we moved into our new home in Westwood, New Jersey. We were eventually surrounded by great neighbors who all had small children, which further strengthened the neighborhood bonds. Our son, Randy, was born at Hackensack Hospital in Hackensack, New Jersey.

It seemed as though we had just arrived in Westwood when we heard our front doorbell ring for the first time. I curiously opened the door and was greeted by a stranger who introduced himself as Joe Wildebush, a former Army Major and resident of Westwood. I invited him in and he mentioned that he had learned that I was a new resident and that I was employed by the federal government. He immediately impressed me as being a friendly and patriotic individual, so I listened carefully to what he had to say.

He said that he was a member of the Pascack Valley Association, which was a group of volunteers determined to build a hospital in Westwood. He wondered if I would be willing to be his first fundraising captain. Without hesitation, I accepted. Our group of volunteers continued to grow as did the contributions from the majority of the people throughout the Pascack Valley. As a result of this generous financial assistance, excavation began in the mid-1950s on some acreage of land on Old Hook Road of what is known today as Hackensack University Medical Center North at Pascack Valley. Our youngest daughter, Cathy, was born there. Looking back, I realize that the efforts to build the hospital was a shining example of the American spirit in which many people selflessly come together to create something larger than themselves.

Community Involvement

My experience in helping to build the hospital was a lesson for me in the value of community – and, the obligation to become personally involved in doing everything that I could to strengthen it. As a relative newcomer to Westwood and having played a rather minor role in what eventually became a hospital, I felt that there was need of a gathering place for children of grammar and high school age. We needed a place where our children could grow in an environment that promoted both their healthy well-being and their civic responsibility.

I decided that if President Kennedy could begin efforts to put a man on the moon, I could begin efforts to put a new swim club in Westwood. After learning that new swim clubs had been established nearby, I went to see them and learned as much as I could. Now, it was time to build a team.

Many people volunteered. We formed the first Board of Trustees for the Westwood Swim Club, Fred Behrends, Claude Blanchard, Charlie Bellon, Dr. Bill Burke, Frank Cameron, Al Chestone, Bill Deegan, Ed Mooney, Bob O'Neill Patricia Procak and Bob Rypkema. Bill Clifford, a teacher at Fair Lawn High School, became our first manager of the new Westwood Swim Club, which opened in May 1963.

A dedication ceremony was held near poolside, which included several dignitaries, before a gathering of approximately 1,500 people. The total membership on opening day was more than 400 families. It was tremendously rewarding for everyone involved in building the Club to witness how much our community enjoyed their new swim club. Today, more than 40 years later, the Westwood Swim Club is still beautifully maintained and considered to be one of the most attractive swim clubs in New Jersey.

A Turn of Events

The years passed quickly. In 1978, my wife and I began making plans to travel to Torino, Italy to visit four of the Italian sisters, all of whom decided to move from Spinnazola to areas where employment was easily obtained. That summer, however, we were informed that my wife had developed a rare form of cancer, leiomyo sarcoma, that demanded immediate treatment.

We left no stone unturned. We traveled to Wayne University in Detroit and Sloan Kettering in New York where patients had been treated for this type of cancer. But the cancer had spread rapidly. My beloved Marcie died at the age of 52 on January 12, 1980, on the thirty-third anniversary of our first date at Ohio University. Her passing left behind the broken hearts of her five children and husband.

On February 14, 1995, I married a lovely widow, Lorraine Ryan, who had four adult children, Kathie, Nancy, Robert and Maureen, plus 5 of my beautiful children, Lynn, Sue, Tom, Randy and Cathy. We had an instant family of nine adorable adult children all of whom are extremely proud and patriotic Americans. We take great pride in our twenty-two foot flagpole beautifully lighted and situated in the front of our home.

Why have I shared all of this with you?

This has been my story of "What America Means To Me." Our country, yours and mine, has given me so much. I feel so privileged and honored to call myself an American. The mere fact that I was born in this beautiful country is a treasure that I shall forever cherish. Imagine being able to practice one's own religious beliefs without fear of harm. Imagine being able to attend high school and even college if the will and desire are strong enough. Imagine the freedom we have to express ourselves without fear of arrest. Imagine the God-given right to vote for political candidates or causes without interference.

I ask you to imagine that, because so many of our fellow citizens around the world cannot. In so many parts of the world, a person's future is determined by others, often before birth. Not here. Not in America. And that is why so many others want to destroy us.

This is America, a true democracy, a country where people seek asylum as opposed to defection. So here again, the title of this book speaks what your heart should hold and to which your mind should agree. "What America Means To Me." It is my hope that you will be further strengthened in your love for America as you read the following chapters.

The Constitution of a Citizen

A credo as set forth was written by John D. Rockefeller, Jr., which he included in a radio broadcast appeal on behalf of the United Service Organization and the National War Fund on July 8, 1941. In 1962 the credo was inscribed on a plaque in front of Rockefeller Center in Manhattan.

Chapter One

I Believe

John D. Rockefeller, Jr.

I believe in the supreme worth of the individual and in his right to life, liberty, and the pursuit of happiness.

I believe that every right implies a responsibility; every opportunity, an obligation; every possession, a duty.

I believe that the law was made for man and not man for the law; that government is the servant of the people and not their master.

I believe in the dignity of labor, whether with head or hand; that the world owes no man a living but that it owes every man an opportunity to make a living.

I believe that thrift is essential to well ordered living and that economy is a prime requisite of a sound financial structure, whether in government, business or personal affairs.

I believe that truth and justice are fundamental to an enduring social order.

I believe in the sacredness of a promise, that a man's word should be as good as his bond; that character – not wealth or power or position – is of supreme worth.

I believe that the rendering of useful service is the common duty of mankind and that only in the purifying fire of sacrifice is the dross of selfishness consumed and the greatness of the human soul set free.

I believe in an all-wise and all-loving God, named by whatever name, and that the individual's highest fulfillment, greatest happiness, and widest usefulness are to be found in living in harmony with His will.

I believe that love is the greatest thing in the world; that it alone can overcome hate; that right can and will triumph over might.

Chapter Two

The Oath of Allegiance

William Tyler Page

I believe in the United States of America as a Government of the people, by the people, for the people, whose just powers are derived from the consent of the governed; a democracy in a republic; a sovereign Nation of many sovereign States; a perfect union, one and inseparable; established upon those principles of freedom, equality, justice, and humanity for which American patriots sacrificed their lives and fortunes. I therefore believe it my duty to my country to love it, to support its Constitution, to obey its laws, to respect its flag, and to defend it against all enemies.

The Oath of Citizenship

I hereby declare, on oath, that I absolutely and entirely renounce and abjure all allegiance and fidelity to any foreign prince, potentate, state, or sovereignty of whom or which I have heretofore been a subject or citizen; that I will support and defend the Constitution and laws of the United States of America against all enemies, foreign and domestic; that I will bear true faith and allegiance to the same; that I will bear arms on behalf of the United States when required by law; that I will perform noncombatant service in the Armed Forces of the United States when required by the law; that I will perform work of national importance under civilian direction when required by the law; and that I take this obligation freely without any mental reservation or purpose of evasion; so help me God.

Mr. Peter Ferrara, the author of the following article, has worked as an Associate Professor of Law at George Mason University School of Law. He was an Associate Deputy Attorney General 1992-93; is a Senior Fellow of the Caro Institute; Senior Fellow, Heritage Foundation, and is associated with the Institute of Policy Innovation and numerous other organizations.

Chapter Three

What Is An American?

Peter Ferrara

There was actually a report that someone in Pakistan had published in a newspaper there an offer of a reward to anyone who killed an American, any American.

So I just thought I would write to let them know what an American is, so they would know when they found one.

An American is English…or French, or Italian, Irish, German, Spanish, Polish, Russian or Greek. An American may also be African, Indian, Chinese, Japanese, Australian, Iranian, Asian, or Arab, or Pakistani, or Afghan.

An American is Christian, or he could be Jewish, or Buddhist, or Muslim. In fact, there are more Muslims in America than in Afghanistan. The only difference is that in America they are free to worship as each of them choose.

An American is also free to believe in no religion. For that he will answer only to God, not to the government, or to armed thugs claiming to speak for the government and for God.

An American is from the most prosperous land in the history of the world. The root of that prosperity can be found in the Declaration of Independence, which recognizes the God-given right of each man and woman to the pursuit of happiness.

An American is generous. Americans have helped out just about every other nation in the world in their time of need. When Afghanistan was overrun by the Soviet army 20 years ago, Americans came with arms and supplies to enable the people to win back their country. As of the morning of September 11, Americans had given more than any other nation to the poor in Afghanistan.

An American does not have to obey the mad ravings of ignorant, ungodly cruel, old men. American men will not be fooled into giving up their lives to kill innocent people, so that these foolish old men may hold on to power. American women are free to show their beautiful faces to the world, as each of them choose.

An American is free to criticize his government's officials when they are wrong, in his or her own opinion. Then he is free to replace them, by majority vote.

Americans welcome people from all lands, all cultures, all religions, because they are not afraid. They are not afraid that their history, their religion, their beliefs, will be overrun, or forgotten. That is because they know they are free to hold to their religion, their beliefs, their history, as each of them choose.

And just as Americans welcome all, they enjoy the best that everyone has to bring, from all over the world. The best science, the best technology, the best products, the best books, the best music, the best food, the best athletes.

Americans welcome the best, but they also welcome the least. The nation symbol of America welcomes your tired and your poor, the wretched refuse of your teeming shores, the homeless, tempest tossed.

These in fact are the people who built America. Many of them were working in the Twin Towers on the morning of September 11, earning a better life for their families.

So you can try to kill an American if you must. Hitler did. So did General Tojo and Stalin and Mao Tse-Tung, and every bloodthirsty tyrant in the history of the world.

But in doing so you would just be killing yourself. Because Americans are not a particular people from a particular place. They are the embodiment of the human spirit of freedom. Everyone who holds to that spirit, everywhere, is an American.

So look around you. You may find more Americans in your land than you thought were there. One day they will rise up and overthrow the old, ignorant, tired tyrants that trouble too many lands. Then those lands too will join the community of free and prosperous nations.

And America will welcome them.

The following article was written by the Honorable Lee Hamilton, former Congressman representing the State of Indiana, who was also the Vice Chairman of the 9/11 Commission in Washington, D.C. Mr. Hamilton serves as the President and Director of the Woodrow Wilson International Center for Scholars in Washington, D.C., and is the Director of the Center on Congress at Indiana University.

Chapter Four

What Does It Mean to Be an American Citizen?

The Hon. Lee H. Hamilton

We are here today because the success of any democracy is determined by the participation of its citizens.

Lincoln asked whether a nation devoted to the values of liberty, equality, justice and opportunity "so conceived . . . can long endure."

In these words, he told us a truth about our democracy – that its survival is never guaranteed, and that its success demands wisdom, action and even vigilance from American citizens.

Thus, I focus my remarks today on the basic question: what does it mean to be an American citizen?

What do we owe?

First, what do we – as American citizens – owe?

We begin with gratitude. As many have said, the joy of being an American is the joy of freedom and opportunity.

We have been bequeathed freedom, justice and opportunity from the deeds and commitments – even the spilled blood – of Americans who came before us.

We did not earn the inheritance. This nation of unequaled wealth and power, of freedom and opportunity, was given to us.

But no matter how rich and powerful it becomes, America is not – and never will be – a finished project. It is always aborting. You and I are handed a work in progress – one that can evolve for good or for ill.

American democracy makes a wager on its citizens. The deal is simple – with freedom comes obligation, with liberty comes duty. If that deal is not kept, democracy is threatened.

Lincoln said at Gettysburg: "It is for us the living, rather, to be dedicated here to the unfinished work which they who fought here have thus far so nobly advanced." He spoke of a "new birth of freedom" so that government of, by and for the people would not perish.

You and I must learn – and we must teach our young – the words we live by: the Constitution, the Declaration of Independence, and the other grand documents of American history. And we must learn and teach about the institutions that bring life and permanence to these words and deeds so familiar to us, so that they may fulfill Lincoln's charge.

Democracy is not fixed like a monarchy. It is dynamic. Democracy reflects the will – and above all the action – of each generation of American citizens.

So what do we owe? As Americans we owe a profound debt of gratitude for the actions of those who preceded us, and we owe those who will follow an America that is even greater and more beautiful than it was transmitted to us.

Why are we concerned?

But I am concerned, as I know you are. Why are we concerned?

We are concerned because too many Americans lack a basic understanding of our democracy – our institutions, our representative democracy, our obligation to those who came before, and what each of us can and must do to preserve the blessings of liberty.

A multitude of surveys confirm our concerns. But we don't even need to look at surveys or statistics to know that political participation and civic engagement is down basically across the board. People are voting less; paying less attention to their civic responsibility; ignoring the great lessons of the American experiment; participating less and complaining more.

There is a se Indiana who – when asked nse, particularly among many young people, that being an American citizen is no big deal, with no obligation attached to it – an endeavor not particularly worthy of their time and talent. I know of young people in about the meaning of Memorial Day – respond by saying that it is the day that pools are opened, or the occasion for the Indianapolis 500 auto race.

All of us are aware of a disconnect between people and their elected representatives. People do not trust them. People think they do the bidding of powerful interests. People think they are not relevant to their day-to-day lives. People think that citizenship is hollow.

You and I are concerned because we know that if we are apathetic, passive, and cynical about our democracy, then we will invite leaders who abuse power. There is an old observation: a society of sheep must in time beget a government of wolves.

You and I are concerned because we stand on a precipice. If American citizens increasingly become disengaged, then the entire American democratic enterprise is at risk. Indeed, sometimes I wonder about whether our democracy can continue as we know it if civic participation continues to decline as it has.

Why engage?

Why should you and I and others engage in civic activity?

We have plenty of important things to worry about – doing our jobs, paying our bills, taking care of our families. No doubt, these private interests are civic virtues in their own right.

We are good – in this country – at speaking out for and protecting our individual interest. But all of us can benefit from giving at least some of our attention to advancing the public interest, or – as the founding fathers called it – the common good.

Look around you. Many things need to be done in your community and country. Perhaps you are upset by the actions of your representative. Or the school that your children attend. Or the quality of your health care. Or the conditions of the roads that you drive on. Or even our nation's foreign policy.

Don't misunderstand me. Tending your own business and the affairs of your family is important. But civic engagement is your way of influencing for the better your neighborhood, community, state and nation. If you and I become involved our cynicism will dissipate and our morale improve. We may even see life become better, richer, and fuller for our fellow citizens.

I know people who vote, walk out of the booth, and say and believe that their civic duty has been fully discharged. Voting is important – but not enough. Do you know who does not disengage when the voting is done? Interest groups. They begin their work the day after an election – they know that's when the real work begins. They know it and so should the rest of us.

If you are upset about the influence exerted by special interests; if you are upset about the actions of a public official; if you are upset about the condition of your local school; even if you are upset about a pothole in front of your house – civic engagement is a way of taking action to make your corner of the world better. What do we have on our agenda that is more important?

The key to good governance is simple: it is to hold power accountable. Civic engagement does just that. We engage because it improves our democracy, and it is the only way to make our government responsive to the people.

What can we do?

How, then, do we engage?

If you ask them, most Americans want to be better people living in better communities, a better state, and a better nation. Often, they want to become involved but don't know how – don't know where to go, whom to talk to, what to do.

Thus the job of civic education is not complete if we teach only its importance; we must be shown how to engage, how to participate, how to get off the sidelines and into the action.

This may seem overwhelming at first. But I like the attitude of the builder who said: "I cannot solve the world's problems, but I can help build this house."

A constituent of mine was a diabetic. He approached me one day many years ago because he had no idea what was in the food on sale at the grocery store, and his health depended upon it.

But he did more than just talk to me. He spoke around the community to whomever would listen; visited and wrote letters to all kinds of officials – county commissioners, state legislators, other members of Congress. Thanks to him, and many people of like mind and action, consumers now have meaningful labels on the food that they buy.

We would all like to engage to resolve the big problem. Fixing health care. Saving social security. Changing the tax code. Defending our nation against its enemies. Some of us have those opportunities, but most of us don't.

All of us can engage most effectively through small, incremental changes. A school is rebuilt. Ramps for the handicapped are carved into street corners. A safety signal goes up in a dangerous intersection. A worthy, young disadvantaged student enters medical school. A young woman steps into the world with more opportunity than her mother.

These are not insignificant examples. They save and improve lives and communities. The actions of my constituent and countless American citizens like him made many American lives healthier. This is the wellspring of our American democracy – countless small actions that make a better nation.

We engage by looking around us, seeing something that needs fixing, and doing something about it:

> - We can stay more informed about issues in our own communities, as well as the issues of the state and nation.

- We can run for elective office or work for candidates of our choice.

- We can vote in elections and hold each of our representatives accountable – from the president on down to a town council or commissioner.

- We can join institutions of service – be it the peace corps, the armed services, Americorps, or local uniformed services.

- We can volunteer for charitable causes and organizations.

- We can join the sometimes messy, rough and tumble dialogue of democracy by writing letters to local papers or elected officials, asking questions or advocating positions.

- We can give speeches or ask questions why things cannot be better across the street or across the world.

- We can organize petition drives or letter writing campaigns.

- We can join – or begin – organizations that reflect our views and enlarge our collective voice.

If you know your community – the problems that need addressing: the different kinds of people (not just the people like you); the issues; who is in charge; who has the power to get a message out; who can assemble people together – I can assure you, you will engage. Set goals; craft messages; organize; and – when successful – share the credit.

Civic engagement is the greatest antidote for cynicism; it is also a great – maybe the best – lesson of democracy.

When we become engaged in community life we no longer feel distant from the centers of power and decision-making. We come to understand our own communities, and appreciate how we can influence change. Perhaps most important, we gain an appreciation for the hard work of democracy – how to understand different points of view and forge a consensus behind a course of action towards a solution in a complex, busy and diverse society.

If we engage, we lessen the distance between ourselves and those who govern. And we gain understanding and appreciation for our country that can only make it – and the ongoing experiment of American democracy – stronger.

Conclusion

You and I believe that democracy is the most worthy form of government. And we know that democracy cannot thrive – indeed, cannot exist – without the active participation of citizens.

So we must get into our bones the ideas of representative democracy: the consent of the governed, the institutions of democracy in our nation, the necessity of participation, and the avenues for action that are open to all of us.

Our engagement brings out the very best within us. Our nation demands not only our competence, but also our passion.

President Kennedy's words resonate through the years: "In your hands, my fellow citizens, more than mine, will rest the final success or failure of our course . . . Ask not what your country can do for you, ask what you can do for your country."

I cherish the citizen who says: I belong here, I have a role to play; I have a contribution to make.

What does it mean to be an American citizen? It means that we are blessed to be part of this nation; we are concerned about a shortage of civic awareness and engagement; and we should act to effect meaningful change and accountable government through countless avenues for civic action. Above all, it means we are responsible for tending to our own democracy, making it work for all and transmitting it to our children better than we inherited it.

You accept the responsibility of an American citizen. Fortunately there are many more Americans like you – but not enough. Our charge is to spread this message anew to all Americans.

Land That I Love

Mr. Elie Wiesel is the author of the following article, "The America I Love." Mr. Wiesel, who became a U.S. citizen in 1963, was born in Sighet, Transylvania (Romania). He won the Nobel Peace Prize in 1986. He is a distinguished professor of Judaic Studies at the City College of New York and a professor in the humanities at Boston University.

<u>Chapter Five</u>

The America I Love

Elie Wiesel

The day I received American citizenship was a turning point in my life. I had ceased to be stateless. Until then, unprotected by any government and unwanted by any society, the Jew in me was overcome by a feeling of pride mixed with gratitude.

From that day on, I felt privileged to belong to a country which, for two centuries, has stood as a living symbol of all that is charitable and decent to victims of injustice everywhere – a country in which every person is entitled to dream of happiness, peace and liberty; where those who have are taught to give back.

In America, compassion for the refugee and respect for the other still have biblical connotations.

Grandiloquent words used for public oratory? Even now, as America is in the midst of puzzling uncertainty and understandable introspection because of tragic events in Iraq, these words reflect my personal belief. For I cannot forget another day that remains alive in my memory: April 11, 1945.

That day I encountered the first American soldiers in the Buchenwald concentration camp. I remember them well. Bewildered, disbelieving, they walked around the place, hell on earth, where our destiny had been played out. They looked at us, just liberated, and did not know what to do or say. Survivors snatched from the dark throes of death, we were empty of all hope – too weak, too emaciated to hug them or even speak to them. Like lost children, the American soldiers wept and wept with rage and sadness. And we received their tears as if they were heartrending offerings from a wounded and generous humanity.

Ever since that encounter, I cannot repress my emotion before the flag and the uniform – anything that represents American heroism in battle. That is especially true on July Fourth. I re-read the Declaration of Independence, a document sanctified by the passion of a nation's thirst for justice and sovereignty, forever admiring both its moral content and majestic intonation. Opposition in all its forms, defense of all human liberties, celebration of what is right in social intercourse: All this and much more is in that text, which today has special meaning.

Granted, U.S. history has gone through severe trials, of which anti-black racism was the most scandalous and depressing. I happened to witness it in the late Fifties, as I traveled through the South. What did I feel? Shame. Yes, shame for being white. What made it worse was the realization that, at that time, racism was the law, thus making the law itself immoral and unjust.

Still, my generation was lucky to see the downfall of prejudice in many of its forms. True, it took much pain and protest for that law to be changed, but it was. Today, while fanatically stubborn racists are still around, some of them vocal, racism as such has vanished from the American scene. That is true of anti-Semitism too. Jew-haters still exist here and there, but organized anti-Semitism does not – unlike in Europe, where it has been growing with disturbing speed.

As a great power, America has always seemed concerned with other people's welfare, especially in Europe. Twice in the 20th century, it saved the "Old World" from dictatorship and tyranny.

America understands that a nation is great not because its economy is flourishing or its army invincible but because its ideals are loftier. Hence America's desire to help those who have lost their freedom to conquer it again. America's credo might read as follows: For an individual, as for a nation, to be free is an admirable duty – but to help others become free is even more admirable.

Some skeptics may object: But what about Vietnam? And Cambodia? And the support some administrations gave to corrupt regimes in Africa or the Middle East? And the occupation of Iraq? Did we go wrong – and if so, where?

And what are we to make of the despicable, abominable "interrogation methods" used on Iraqi prisoners of war by a few soldiers (but even a few are too many) in Iraqi military prisons?

Well, one could say that no nation is composed of saints alone. None is sheltered from mistakes or misdeeds. All have their Cain and Abel. It takes vision and courage to undergo serious soul-searching and to favor moral conscience over political expediency. And America, in extreme situations, is endowed with both. America is always ready to learn from its mishaps. Self-criticism remains its second nature.

Not surprising, some Europeans do not share such views. In extreme left-wing political and intellectual circles, suspicion and distrust toward America is the order of the day. They deride America's motives for its military interventions, particularly in Iraq. They say: It's just money. As if America went to war only to please the oil-rich capitalists.

They are wrong. America went to war to liberate a population too long subjected to terror and death.

We see in newspapers and magazines and on television screens the mass graves and torture chambers imposed by Saddam Hussein and his accomplices. One cannot but feel grateful to the young Americans who leave their families, some to lose their lives, in order to bring to Iraq the first rays of hope – without which no people can imagine the happiness of welcoming freedom.

Hope is a key word in the vocabulary of men and women like myself and so many others who discovered in America the strength to overcome cynicism and despair. Remember the legendary Pandora's box? It is filled with implacable, terrifying curses.

Mr. Dinesh D'Souza is a world renowned author who graduated Phi Beta Kappa from Dartmouth College in 1983. He was the senior domestic policy analyst of the White House during the Reagan administration from 1987 to 1988. He has authored numerous books, one in particular that is entitled, "What's So Great About America," an excerpt of which appears on the following pages.

Chapter Six

What's So Great About America

(Excerpts)

Dinesh D'Souza

In the aftermath of the 9/11 terrorist attack, we have heard a great deal about "why they hate us" and about why America is so bad. We've endured lengthy lectures about America's history of slavery, about the effects of American foreign policy, about the materialism of American life, and about the excesses of American culture. In the view of many critics at home and abroad, America can do no right.

This indictment, which undermines the patriotism of Americans, is based on a narrow and distorted understanding of America. It exaggerates America's faults, and it ignores what is good and even great about America. As an immigrant who has chosen to become a U.S. citizen, I feel especially qualified to say what is special about this country. Having grown up in a different society – in my case, Mumbai, India – I am not only able to identify aspects of America that are invisible to people who have always lived here, but I am also acutely conscious of the daily blessings I enjoy in America.

Here, then, is my list of the 10 great things about America.

(1) America provides an amazingly good life for the ordinary guy: Rich people live well everywhere. But what distinguishes America is that it provides an incomparably high standard of living for the "commonman." We now live in a country where construction workers regularly pay $4 for a nonfat latte, where maids drive nice cars, and where plumbers take their families on vacation to Europe.

Indeed newcomers to the United States are struck by the amenities enjoyed by "poor" people in the United States. This fact was dramatized in the 1980s when CBS television broadcast a documentary, "People Like Us," which was intended to show the miseries of the poor during an ongoing recession.

The Soviet Union also broadcast the documentary, with a view to embarrassing the Reagan administration. But by the testimony of former Soviet leaders, it had the opposite effect. Ordinary people across the Soviet Union saw that the poorest Americans have TV sets, microwave ovens and cars. They arrived at the same perception that I witnessed in an acquaintance of mine from Bombay who has been unsuccessfully trying to move to the United States. I asked him, "Why are you so eager to come to America?" He replied, "I really want to live in a country where the poor people are fat."

(2) America offers more opportunity and social mobility than any other country, including the countries of Europe: America is the only country that has created a population of "self-made tycoons." Only in America could Pierre Omidyar, whose parents are Iranian and who grew up in Paris, have started a company like eBay. Only in America could Vinod Khosla, the son of an Indian army officer, become a leading venture capitalist, the shaper of the technology industry and a billionaire to boot. Admittedly tycoons are not typical, but no country has created a better ladder than America for people to ascend from modest circumstances to success.

(3) Work and trade are respectable in America, which is not true elsewhere: Historically, most cultures have despised the merchant and the laborer, regarding the former as vile and corrupt and the latter as degraded and vulgar. Some cultures, such as that of ancient Greece and medieval Islam, even held it is better to acquire things through plunder than through trade or contract labor. But the American Founders altered this moral hierarchy. They established a society in which the life of the businessman, and of the people who worked for him, would be a noble calling. In the American view, there is nothing vile or degraded about serving your customers either as a CEO or as a waiter. The ordinary life of production and supporting a family is more highly valued in the United States than in any other country. Indeed America is the only country in the world where we call the waiter "sir," as if he were a knight.

(4) America has achieved greater social equality than any other society: True, there are large inequalities of income and wealth in America. In purely economic terms, Europe is more egalitarian. But Americans are socially more equal than any other people, and this is unaffected by economic disparities. Alexis de Tocqueville noticed this egalitarianism a century and a half ago, but it is if anything more prevalent today. For all his riches, Bill Gates could not approach the typical American and say, "Here's a $100 bill. I'll give it to you if you kiss my feet." Most likely the person would tell Mr. Gates where to go. The American view is that the rich guy may have more money, but he isn't in any fundamental sense better than anyone else.

(5) People live longer, fuller lives in America: Although protesters rail against the American version of technological capitalism at trade meetings around the world, in reality the American system has given citizens many more years of life and the means to live more intensely and actively. In 1900, the life expectancy in America was around 50 years; today, it is more than 75 years. Advances in medicine and agriculture are mainly responsible for this change. This extension of the lifespan means more years to enjoy life, more free time to devote to a good cause, and more occasions to do things with the grandchildren. In many countries, people who are old seem to have nothing to do: they just wait to die. In America the old are incredibly vigorous, and people in their 70s pursue the pleasures of life, including remarriage and sexual gratification, with a zeal that I find unnerving.

(6) In America, the destiny of the young is not given to them but created by them. Not long ago, I asked myself, "What would my life have been like if I had never come to the United States?"

If I had remained in India, I would probably have lived my whole life within a 5-mile radius of where I was born. I would undoubtedly have married a woman of my identical religious and socioeconomic background. I would almost certainly have become a medical doctor, or an engineer or a computer programmer. I would have socialized entirely within my ethnic community. I would have a whole set of options that could be predicted in advance; indeed, they would not be very different from what my father believed, or his father before him. In sum, my destiny would to a large degree have been given to me.

In America, I have seen my life take a radically different course. In college, I became interested in literature and politics, and I resolved to make a career as a writer. I married a woman whose ancestry is English, French, Scotch-Irish, German, and American Indian. In my 20s I found myself working as a policy analyst in the White House, even though I was not an American citizen. No other country, I am sure, would have permitted a foreigner to work in its inner citadel of government.

In most countries in the world, your fate and your identity are handed to you; in America, you determine them for yourself. America is a country where you get to write the script of your own life. Your life is like a blank sheet of paper, and you are the artist. This notion of being the architect of your own destiny is the incredibly powerful idea that is behind the worldwide appeal of America. Young people especially find irresistible the prospect of authoring the narrative of their own lives.

(7) America has gone further than any other society in establishing equality of rights: There is nothing distinctively American about slavery or bigotry. Slavery has existed in virtually every culture, and xenophobia, prejudice and discrimination are worldwide phenomena. Western civilization is the only civilization to mount a principled campaign against slavery; no country expended more treasure and blood to get rid of slavery than the United States.

While racism remains a problem in America, this country has made strenuous efforts to eradicate discrimination, even to the extent of enacting policies that give legal preference in university admissions, jobs and government contracts to members of minority groups. Such policies remain controversial, but the point is that it is extremely unlikely that a racist society would have permitted such policies in the first place. And surely African-Americans like Jesse Jackson are vastly better off living in America than they would be if they were to live in, say, Ethiopia or Somalia.

(8) America has found a solution to the problem of religious and ethnic conflict that continues to divide and terrorize much of the world: Visitors to places like New York are amazed to see the way in which Serbs and Croatians, Sikhs and Hindus, Irish Catholics and Irish Protestants, Jews and Palestinians, all seem to work and live together in harmony. How is this possible when the same groups are spearing each other and burning each other's homes in so many places in the world?

The American answer is twofold. First, separate the spheres of religion and government so no religion is given official preference but all are free to practice their faith as they wish. Second, do not extend rights to racial or ethnic groups but only to individuals; in this way, all are equal in the eyes of the law, opportunity is open to anyone who can take advantage of it, and everybody who embraces the American way of life can "become American."

Of course there are exceptions to these core principles, even in America. Racial preferences are one such exception, which explains why they are controversial. But in general America is the only country in the world that extends full membership to outsiders. The typical American could come to India, live for 40 years, and take Indian citizenship. But he could not "become Indian." He wouldn't see himself that way, nor would most Indians see him that way. In America, by contrast, hundreds of millions have come from far-flung shores and over time they, or at least their children, have in a profound and full sense "become American."

(9) America has the kindest, gentlest foreign policy of any great power in world history: Critics of the U.S. are likely to react to this truth with sputtering outrage. They will point to longstanding American support for a Latin or Middle Eastern despot, or the unjust internment of the Japanese during World War II, or America's reluctance to impose sanctions on South Africa's apartheid regime. However one feels about these particular cases, let us concede to the critics the point that America is not always in the right.

What the critics leave out is the other side of the ledger. Twice in the 20th century, the United States saved the world: first from the Nazi threat, then from Soviet totalitarianism. What would have been the world's fate if America had not existed? After destroying Germany and Japan in World War II, the U.S. proceeded to rebuild both countries, and today they are American allies. Now we are doing the same thing with Afghanistan.

Consider, too, how magnanimous the U.S. has been to the former Soviet Union after its victory in the Cold War. For the most part America is an abstaining superpower: It shows no real interest in conquering and subjugating the rest of the world. (Imagine how the Soviets would have acted if they had won the Cold War.)

On occasion America intervenes to overthrow a tyrannical regime or to halt massive human-rights abuses in another country, but it never stays to rule that country. In Grenada, Haiti and Bosnia, the U.S. got in and then it got out.

Moreover, when America does get into a war, it is supremely careful to avoid targeting civilians and to minimize collateral damage. Even as America bombed the Taliban infrastructure and hideouts, its planes dropped rations of food to avert hardship and starvation of Afghan civilians. What other country does these things?

(10) America, the freest nation on Earth, is also the most virtuous nation on Earth: This point seems counterintuitive, given the amount of conspicuous vulgarity, vice and immorality in America. Indeed some Islamic fundamentalists argue that their regimes are morally superior to the United States because they seek to foster virtue among the citizens. Virtue, these fundamentalists argue, is a higher principle than liberty.

Indeed it is. And let us admit that in a free society, freedom will frequently be used badly. Freedom, by definition, includes the freedom to do good or evil, to act nobly or basely. But if freedom brings out the worst in people, it also brings out the best. The millions of Americans who live decent, praiseworthy lives desire our highest admiration because they have opted for the good when the good is not the only available option. Even amidst the temptations of a rich and free society, they have remained on the straight path. Their virtue has special luster because it is freely chosen.

By contrast, the societies that many Islamic fundamentalists seek would eliminate the possibility of virtue. If the supply of virtue is insufficient in a free society like America, it is almost nonexistent in an unfree society like Iran. The reason is that coerced virtues are not virtues at all.

Consider the woman who is required to wear a veil. There is no modesty in this, because she is being compelled. Compulsion cannot produce virtue, it can only produce the outward semblance of virtue. Thus a free society like America is not merely more prosperous, more varied, more peaceful, and more tolerant – it is also morally superior to the theocratic and authoritarian regimes that America's enemies advocate.

"To make us love our country," Edmund Burke once said, "our country ought to be lovely." Burke's point is that we should love our country not just because it is ours, but also because it is good. America is far from perfect, and there is lots of room for improvement. Despite its flaws, however, the American life as it is lived today is the best life our world has to offer. Ultimately America is worthy of our love and sacrifice because, more than any other society, it makes possible the good life and the life that is good.

Although much of America is immersed in Rousseau's ethic of authenticity, there are sizable segments of the culture that have not been infiltrated by it. The firefighters and policemen who raced into the burning towers of the World Trade Center showed that their lives were dedicated to something higher than "self-fulfillment." The same can be said of Todd Beamer and his fellow passengers who forced the terrorists to crash United Airlines Flight 93 in the woods of western Pennsylvania rather than flying on to Camp David or the White House. Authenticity, thank God, is not the operating principle of the U.S. military. America's enemies should not expect to do battle against the Starbucks guy. The military has its own culture, which is closer to that of the firefighters and policemen, and also bears an affinity with the culture of the "greatest generation." Only now are those Americans who grew up during the 1960s coming to appreciate the virtues – indeed the indispensability – of this older, sturdier culture of courage, nobility, and sacrifice. It is this culture that will protect the liberties of all Americans, including that of the Starbucks guy.

As the American founders knew, America is a new kind of society that produces a new kind of human being. That human being – confident, self-reliant, tolerant, generous, future oriented – is a vast improvement over the wretched, servile, fatalistic, and intolerant human being that traditional societies have always produced, and that Islamic societies produce now. In America, the life we are given is not as important as the life we make. Ultimately, America is worthy of our love and sacrifice because, more than any other society, it makes possible the good life, and the life that is good.

America is the greatest, freest, and most decent society in existence. It is an oasis of goodness in a desert of cynicism and barbarism. This country, once an experiment unique in the world, is now the last best hope for the world. By making sacrifices for America, and by our willingness to die for her, we bind ourselves by invisible cords to those great patriots who fought at Yorktown, Gettysburg, and Iwo Jima and we prove ourselves worthy of the blessings of freedom. By defeating the terrorist threat posed by Islamic fundamentalism, we can protect the American way of life while once again redeeming humanity from a global menace. History will view America as a great gift to the world, a gift that Americans today must preserve and cherish.

The following page was written and delivered by one of the most outstanding Canadian Radio Journalists, Gordon Sinclair. It was aired on June 5, 1973, from Toronto during his regular radio series, "Let's Be Personal." On this particular day, Mr. Sinclair's topic was "The Americans," and it was heard around the world. As a result, the bridge of friendship between Canada and the United States was further strengthened. Mr. Sinclair was an honorary citizen of North Carolina, but unfortunately died of a heart attack on May 17, 1984.

On February 1, 2007, his granddaughter, Connie Sinclair, granted me permission to incorporate "The Americans" in this book. At that time she wrote to me, "Al, go ahead and use Grandpa's 'Americans.' He'd be pleased it's still making the rounds."

Chapter Seven

The Americans

Gordon Sinclair

The United States dollar took another pounding on German, French and British exchanges this morning, hitting the lowest point ever known in West Germany. It has declined there by 41% since 1971 and this Canadian thinks it is time to speak up for the Americans as the most generous and possibly the least-appreciated people in all the world.

As long as sixty years ago, when I first started to read newspapers, I read of floods on the Yellow River and the Yangtse. Well, Who rushed in with men and money to help? The Americans did, that's who.

They have helped control floods on the Nile, the Amazon, the Ganges and the Niger. Today, the rich bottom land of the Mississippi is under water and no foreign land has sent a dollar to help. Germany, Japan and, to a lesser extent, Britain and Italy, were lifted out of the debris of war by the Americans who poured in billions of dollars and forgave other billions in debts. None of those countries is today paying even the interest on its remaining debts to the United States.

When the franc was in danger of collapsing in 1956, it was the Americans who propped it up and their reward was to be insulted and swindled on the streets of Paris. And I was there. I saw that.

When distant cities are hit by earthquakes, it is the United States that hurries into help… Managua, Nicaragua, is one of the most recent examples. So far this spring, 59 American communities have been flattened by tornadoes. Nobody has helped.

The Marshall Plan… the Truman Policy… all pumped billions upon billions of dollars into discouraged countries. And now, newspapers in those countries are writing about the decadent war-mongering Americans.

I'd like to see one of those countries that is gloating over the erosion of the United States dollar build its own airplanes.

Come on… let's hear it! Does any other country in the world have a plane to equal the Boeing Jumbo Jet, the Lockheed Tristar or the Douglas 10? If so, why don't they fly them? Why do all international lines except Russia fly American planes? Why does no other land on earth even consider putting a man or a woman on the moon?

You talk about Japanese technocracy and you get radios. You talk about German technocracy and you get automobiles. You talk about American technocracy and you find men on the moon, not once, but several times… and safely home again. You talk about scandals and the Americans put theirs right in the store window for everybody to look at. Even the draft dodgers are not pursued and hounded. They are right here on our streets in Toronto, most of them… unless they are breaking Canadian laws… are getting American dollars from Ma and Pa at home to spend here.

When the Americans get out of this bind… as they will… who could blame them if they said 'the hell with the rest of the world.' Let someone else buy the bonds, let someone else build or repair foreign dams or design foreign buildings that won't shake apart in earthquakes.

When the railways of France, Germany and India were breaking down through age, it was the Americans who rebuilt them. When the Pennsylvania Railroad and the New York Central went broke, nobody loaned them an old caboose. Both of them are still broke. I can name to you 5,000 times when the Americans raced to the help of other people in trouble.

Can you name to me even one time when someone else raced to the Americans in trouble? I don't think there was outside help even during the San Francisco earthquake.

Our neighbours have faced it alone and I am one Canadian who is damned tired of hearing them kicked around. They will come out of this thing with their flag high. And when they do, they are entitled to thumb their noses at the lands that are gloating over their present troubles.

I hope Canada is not one of these. But there are many smug, self-righteous Canadians. And finally, the American Red Cross was told at its 48th Annual meeting in New Orleans this morning that it was broke.

Chapter Eight

Ode To America

Cornel Nistorescu

Journalist, Bucharest, Romania
(Appeared in the Romanian newspaper, Evenimentul Zilei
on Sept. 24, 2002)

Why are Americans so united? They don't resemble one another even if you paint them! They speak all the languages of the world and form an astonishing mixture of civilizations. Some of them are nearly extinct, others are incompatible with one another, and in matters of religious beliefs, not even God can count how many they are.

Still, the American tragedy turned three hundred million people into a hand put on the heart. Nobody rushed to accuse the White House, the army, the secret services that they are only a bunch of losers. Nobody rushed to empty their bank accounts. Nobody rushed on the streets nearby to gape about. The Americans volunteered to donate blood and to give a helping hand. After the first moments of panic, they raised the flag on the smoking ruins, putting on T-shirts, caps and ties in the colors of the national flag. They placed flags on buildings and cars as if in every place and on every car a minister or the president was passing. On every occasion they started singing their traditional song: "God Bless America!"

Silent as a rock, I watched the charity concert broadcast on Saturday once, twice, three times, on different TV channels. There were Clint Eastwood, Willie

Nelson, Robert de Niro, Julia Roberts, Cassius Clay, Jack Nicholson, Bruce Springsteen, Sylvester Stallone, James Wood, and many others whom no film or producers could ever bring together. The American's solidarity spirit turned them into a choir. Actually, choir is not the word. What you could hear was the heavy artillery of the American soul. What neither George W. Bush, nor Bill Clinton, nor Colin Powell could say without facing the risk of stumbling over words and sounds, was being heard in a great and unmistakable way in this charity concert.

I don't know how it happened that all this obsessive singing of America didn't sound croaky, nationalist, or ostentatious! It made you green with envy because you weren't able to sing for your country without running the risk of being considered chauvinist, ridiculous, or suspected of who-knows-what mean interests.

I watched the live broadcast and the rerun of its rerun for hours listening to the story of the guy who went down one hundred floors with a woman in a wheelchair without knowing who she was, or of the Californian hockey player, who fought with the terrorists and prevented the plane from hitting a target that would have killed other hundreds or thousands of people. How on earth were they able to bow before a fellow human?

Imperceptibly, with every word and musical note, the memory of some turned into a modern myth of tragic heroes. And with every phone call, millions and millions of dollars were put in a collection aimed at rewarding not a man or a family, but a spirit which nothing can buy.

What on earth can unite the Americans in such a way? Their land? Their galloping history? Their economic power? Money? I tried for hours to find an answer, humming songs and murmuring phrases with risk of sounding like commonplaces. I thought things over, but I reached only one conclusion.

Only freedom can work such miracles!

In God We Trust

Rick Scarborough has issued a call to Christian involvement in his book entitled, "Enough is Enough," a chapter of which has been set forth with permission. Rick Scarborough has been an evangelist and pastor since 1969. In 1996, he founded "Vision America," a national ministry dedicated to mobilizing pastors into the civil government arena.

<u>Chapter Nine</u>

Enough is Enough

(Excerpt)

Rick Scarborough

American Institutions Were Built on Biblical Truth

In Washington's last address to the Congress, he made an impacting statement regarding his personal view of the role of the Bible and government. "It is impossible to rightly govern the world without God and the Bible…" "It is impossible to govern the universe without the aid of a supreme Being." George Washington understood the importance of God's protection being placed around the nation: "Let us unite in imploring the Supreme Ruler of nations to spread his holy protection over these United States."

The name of American, which belongs to you, in your national capacity, must always exalt the just pride of patriotism, more than any appellation derived from local discriminations. With slight shades of difference, you have same religion, manners, habits and political principles… Of all the dispositions and habits which led to political prosperity, religion and morality are indispensable supports.

> In vain would that man claim the tribute of patriotism, who should labor to subvert these great pillars of human happiness, these firmest props of the duties of men and citizens. The mere

politician, equally with the pious man, ought to respect and to cherish them. A volume could not trace all their connections with private and public felicity. Let it simply be asked where is the security for prosperity, for reputation, for life, if the sense of religious obligation desert the oaths, which are the instruments of investigation in the Courts of Justice?

And let us with caution indulge the supposition, that morality can be maintained without religion. Whatever may be conceded to the influence of refined education on minds of peculiar structure, reason and experience both forbid us to expect that national morality can prevail in exclusion of religious principle. Tis substantially true, that virtue or morality is a necessary spring of popular government . . . Can it not be that Providence has not connected the permanent felicity of a nation with its virtue?

These insightful words spoken on September 19, 1796, were words of prophecy. For the better part of two centuries, this nation maintained a clear cultural identity. The name, "American," applied to a people who held the same religion, habits and political principles, with only shades of difference. How far we have fallen as a nation! When are we going to finally decide "Enough is Enough?"

Author's Comment:

To further support George Washington's personal view of the role of the Bible and government, I wish to draw the reader's attention to a statement written by a former justice of the U.S. Supreme Court:

Our laws and our institutions must necessarily be based upon and embody the teachings of the Redeemer of mankind. It is impossible that it should be otherwise, and in this sense and to this extent our civilization and our institutions are emphatically Christian.

> Justice Josiah Brewer
> United States Supreme Court, Feb 29, 1892
> Church of the Holy Trinity v. United States

The following article was written by Hilmar von Campe, who was listed in the 1992 "International Who's Who of Intellectuals." He has authored several books and has made both radio and TV appearances. He served in the German army during World War II and was a prisoner of war in Yugoslavia, from where he staged a daring escape in 1945, crossing seven borders to freedom.

He lived through the years of Nazi power and propaganda in Germany as a child and then as a soldier. He is a graduate of the University of Hamburg and has traveled the world investigating political and social conditions. The loss of his father in a Soviet Concentration Camp, the destruction of Germany and the expulsion from his home in Eastern Europe had a profound impact on his life. His most recent book is entitled, *Defeating the Totalitarian Lie*

Chapter Ten

The Lost Purpose of History

Hilmar Von Campe

It is about time that America and the Western world go back to their roots in order to understand the nature of our organized enemies, and to defeat them. Such enemies include the Islamic terrorists. The shallowness of our so-called leaders is appalling in that they do not acknowledge this necessity.

Christian teachings include the concept that mankind's history is a moving process that culminates in the Second Coming of Christ and the establishment of the Kingdom of God on earth. Eschatology is the doctrine concerning the "last things" – the final consummation of God's purposes in creation and the final destination of individual souls and all of humanity.

This Christian concept was stolen by the fabricators of materialistic ideologies who replaced the divine link to eternity with a secular culmination in their hate-driven ideologies. The National Socialists, generally called Nazis, had a vision of a German national community and a world run by the master race – they themselves. The final destination for international socialists, the communist Marxists/Leninists, was defined as a global socialist and classless society, which, however, would be a totalitarian system run by godless functionaries. The destination of radical Islam is a Muslim world where the Muftis rule and no other religion exists. Those who kill unbelievers refusing to convert to Islam are promised awards in paradise. Followers of these three godless ideologies consider themselves part of a process in which they change the direction of history to reach the final destination. They are groomed to invest their whole existence and life into achieving victory for their ideology. This is also a perversion of the Christian teaching that Almighty God wants the whole person and not just some part.

The West has lost the concept that history is meant to be a movement of humanity toward God. It has eliminated Christian teachings as irrelevant for the political process and has reduced the Christian message to a purely personal affair. American and Western Christians love their comfort and do not want to risk heir existence. Western nations and their political and religious leaders, therefore, do not understand the purpose and motives of their ideological enemies, nor do they understand their mindset. They have their own mindset and mistakenly assume that others think as they do. They don't!

This ignorance leads to dangerous political concepts like believing that we have won the Cold War and the Russians now are our democratic allies. The reality, however, is different. Gorbachev, Putin and all the others are the same dedicated communists as always, but have only put democratic labels on their outside.

Similarly fatal is to believe that the Arabic Palestinians are the real owners of the land that is "occupied" by Israel, and that peace will be achieved if they get their own government and are given more of "their" land. Ownership and "occupation" is the other way around – Arabs live on land which already thousands of years ago was part of an Israeli state.

Even more dangerous for America is the attempt to form a North American Community. It would destroy our sovereignty and uniqueness, make us a multicultural country with economic reasoning and cripple our mission to carry freedom to the last corner of the world. It is that task which links this nation to the historic movement of humanity toward God. But it needs more than military power.

Dr. Zuhdi Jasser is founder and board chairman of the American Islamic Forum for Democracy (AIFD). A former U.S. Navy Lieutenant Commander, he served in the U.S. Navy as a medical officer from 1988–99. He finished his military service as a Lieutenant Commander with an Honorable Discharge in 1999 and is now in the private practice of internal medicine and nuclear cardiology in Phoenix, Arizona.

This excerpt of an e-note is based on his September 26 talk as the 12th Annual Templeton Lecture on Religion and World Affairs. It and the other Templeton lectures are available online at www.fpri.org/education/templetonlecture.html.

<u>Chapter Eleven</u>

Americanism vs. Islamism:
A Personal Perspective
12th Annual Templeton Lecture on
Religion and World Affairs

(Excerpt)

Dr. Zuhdi Jasser

Once in the early 1990s, on leave from the military, I went to an Islamic medical association meeting. One of the only other Muslim medical officers was the head of endocrinology at Bethesda. He and I were going to present a paper on hormonal regulation and some endocrine issues at the Islamic Medical Association, which was being held in conjunction with the Islamic Society of North America annual conference. I had never been to a meeting of ISNA, the largest Muslim organization in America. Its annual meetings are attended by 15,000-30,000 Muslim activists. The keynote address was given by Siraj Wahhaj, Imam of Al-Taqwa Mosque in Brooklyn, New York, who was originally with the Nation of Islam and then converted to Sunni Islam. I was pulled into listening to this magnetic speaker, until he began talking about the constitution. He picked up the Quran and said "You know, I was on an airplane and imagine, a Jewish passenger sitting next to me asked me about the Quran I was reading—if Muslims became a majority in America, would we replace the U.S. constitution with the Quran." He laughed and said, "Can you imagine someone wondering if a document made by humans would be superior to a document made by God?"

I got lightheaded, I sat down, and after he was done I went to the Q-and-A microphone and said, "I'm not sure if you understand American law, but you have just violated the Sedition Act as I understand it. You're free to disagree with foreign and domestic policy, but you cannot talk about the overthrow of the U.S. constitution and its replacement by another document." I encouraged other military personnel in the audience to leave, because they were violating their oath to this country. It was in some ways traumatic for me. I had just joined the Navy. But yet they felt that I was overreacting. I feel that it is not overreaction. There are certain things we have to know as a community and as a nation that take priority over other things....

At the end of the day, if we believe that those values they're going to use to drive their ideas are going to be based on morality, that morality has to come from somewhere. If it's not going to come from Islam, then we're going to have to convert over 1 billion people to another faith, and that's not going to work. So that source of values is going to have to be their faith of Islam, which we as Muslims believe is a message from the God of Abraham to Muslims. But that message has to be put in a way that's consistent with modernity and pluralism.

What can we do as a Western society within our community and what can we do, especially for non-Muslims and other organizations, to help this process along and move it along faster than the five hundred years of stagnancy that we've been under?

First, in our own societies, we need to be cautious about permitting parallel societies, parallel courts such as sharia courts where Muslims are given the "freedom" to set up their own legal court system. They would become an incubator for radical Islamism. Canada tried this, and the most vocal voice against sharia courts were Muslim women, even though they were told by the non-Muslims in Canada that "You don't have to, it's voluntary." Once you get swept into this, it's like fighting domestic violence in our own country. We must prevent the establishment of institutions that cater to that and allow the incubation.

Second, we see many examples like the taxicab drivers in Minneapolis who wanted to be separate from the society, not to carry people who were carrying alcohol, to impose their values on the passengers they picked up. Some may say that making a lot out of these issues is an exaggeration—"you need to lighten up." But every opportunity I have to highlight examples, of what in medicine we would call pathegnemonic symptoms, of the pathology of Islamism, I will exploit that. Because *they* are doing the same thing. They are exploiting victimization issues and politics to use what we have now been calling law-fare to get us distracted, to sue individuals who are the biggest threat to their ideas. So that we're all so busy fighting lawsuits such as the flying imams case (the six imams who filed suit against U.S. Airways in March 2007 for having been removed from a flight in November 2006 after behavior that many have called provocative) to distract us, to continue to divide society between Muslim and non-Muslim and to allow the continued inculcation of this Islamist ideology via Muslim collectivism.

A good example is Carver Elementary School in San Diego, which because of the third of its students who are Muslim wanted to move the lunchtime from 12:30 to 1:30 pm so that they could have their prayers. I wrote a column and on CNN talked about the fact that many of us grew up in public elementary schools praying and doing our own practices of faith without asking for the entire school to change its time schedule. You can step away during a break and practice your faith. Certainly I would not want schools to prevent Muslims from praying, they should be given the space to pray if they need it. Because that's a personal faith practice. But once that personal faith practice crosses the line into society and starts changing the schedule of the general society or changing the cost to general society to the taxpayers, as we saw with the footbath incidents where the University of Michigan was paying $30,000 to install footbaths, that crosses the line of the founding principles of America. I don't have a problem with private funding for that if they need it, fine. But not from the taxpayers. For once it comes from the taxpayers, then they should have allotted $30,000 for every other faith group in that university at the same time.

When I was growing up in the 1970s, I don't remember Muslims asking for any of these things. It has almost become a tool of self-segregation and separating Muslims from non-Muslims so that they can continue this issue of minority politics. It's becoming very potent and we have allowed it to take over the debate. It soaks up the bandwidth of American attention instead of allowing us to fight for freedom.

Islamic organizations today have only come to notoriety because of America's fear of terrorism. If terrorism disappeared tomorrow, nobody would care about footbaths, schedules in schools, etc. Focusing on those issues would be the same as if a patient came into my office with lung cancer and I spent my whole time focusing on their cholesterol, headaches, and every other issue except the cancer. The Muslim community for credibility needs to start focusing most of its resources on the root cause of terrorism as a tactic, which is political Islam....

So second, the Muslim community needs to be held accountable to its concept of *umma*. *Umma* is a word that is very prevalent in the Quran. It means "nation" or "community." When an imam talks about *umma*, in Arabic and in his sermons, it is a threatening concept, because you then wonder at what point does an American Muslim follow the needs of the Muslim nation vs. the needs of the American nation to which he or she is a citizen. The Muslim community needs to "de-*umma*tize" itself, to really restrict the mechanism by which the umma is invoked. I would personally limit it to our study of theology and learning about the Quran and scripture; to charity that obviously all of our faiths seek to give; to socialization, obviously marriage within the faith is something all of our faiths try to do; and then last facilitating our hajj, our pilgrimage, and other aspects of practice and spirituality including mosques and community worship.

Third, we need to change the dreams. The dreams of most Muslims today are still wedded, because they have come from oppression and dictatorships, to religion, because the mosque was the last institution where they had a little freedom of speech, as long as they didn't speak against their own government. That's why the Muslim Brotherhood took over the mosques in Syria, and why the Wahhabis were able to spread texts into most of the mosques in the world, at a cost of $80 billion that they spent on spreading the radical word of Wahhabism. They were able to inculcate this literature into a lot of mosques, under the guise of most of these dictatorships.

We need to change those dreams from dreams of the utopian caliphate or Islamic states that bring them supposedly Islamic freedom to dreams of Western, individual freedom, where access to government and society is open to all. Much of the leadership on this must come from Muslim business leaders, who can argue for the kind of education that is needed.

Next, help us establish institutions. The Western enlightenment happened with the establishment of enlightenment institutions, classically liberal institutions that queried the church and government and began to question authority.

Hold some litmus tests and standards for the Muslims you engage with organizationally. They need to recognize Israel as a state, to stand against radical Islamist groups by name, not by theory, tactic, or condemning terrorism, but by name—Hamas, Al Qaeda and other groups. If they don't have the moral courage to name the Saudis, the Syrian government, as an oppressive dictatorship, then you have to wonder where their allegiances are. These types of litmus tests are not being done enough even by our own government and the people they attach themselves to.

We need help in what I would call a *counter-jihad* that is still in its earliest, mitotic cell divisions. There are so many factors affecting the ability of Muslims to really contribute and get involved. One is because of fear—moderates are actually the first to be attacked; because of tribalism, because of the lack of knowledge. There are probably more people in this room who understand sharia than in most of the Muslim groups I've spoken to. That's sad. It's because the reins of understanding intellectual theology in Islam are just given up by most Muslims....

For the eternal gift that is freedom

I am most thankful for the eternal gift which is American liberty and universal religious freedom. I am also thankful to all of those who protect it on the battlefield and in the war of ideas. Nothing protects us more from the terror of militant Islamism than a citizenry empowered by the universal religious freedoms granted by our Constitution and Bill of Rights. I pray that soon far more Muslims will muster the moral courage to vocally, globally, and effectively articulate a preference for this system of liberty over one guided by political Islam. Only then, will we feel a profound increase in American and western security from militant Islamism.

A Patriot's Glance at American History

Chapter Twelve

President Reagan's Farewell Address to the Nation

(Excerpt)
January 11, 1989

…There is a great tradition of warnings in Presidential farewells, and I've got one that's been on my mind for some time. But oddly enough it starts with one of the things I'm proudest of in the past 8 years: the resurgence of national pride that I called the new patriotism. The national feeling is good, but it won't count for much, and it won't last unless it's grounded in thoughtfulness and knowledge.

An informed patriotism is what we want. And are we doing a good enough job teaching our children what America is and what she represents in the long history of the world? Those of us who are over 35 or so years of age grew up in a different America. We were taught, very directly, what it means to be an American. And we absorbed, almost in the air, a love of country and an appreciation of its institutions. If you didn't get these things from your family you got them from the neighborhood, from the father down the street who fought in Korea or the family who lost someone in Anzio. Or you could get a sense of patriotism from school. And if all else failed you could get a sense of patriotism from the popular culture. The movies celebrated democratic values and implicitly reinforced the idea that America was special. TV was like that, too, through the mid-sixties.

But now, we're about to enter the nineties, and some things have changed. Younger parents aren't sure that an unambivalent appreciation of America is the right thing to teach modern children. And as for those who create the popular culture, well-grounded patriotism is no longer the style. Our spirit is back, but we haven't reinstitutionalized it. We've got to do a better job of getting across that America is freedom – freedom of speech, freedom of religion, freedom of enterprise. And freedom is special and rare. It's fragile; it needs production [protection].

So, we've got to teach history based on not what's in fashion but what's important – why the Pilgrims came here, who Jimmy Doolittle was, and what those 30 seconds over Tokyo meant. You know, 4 years ago on the 40th anniversary of D – day, I read a letter from a young woman writing to her late father, who'd fought on Omaha Beach. Her name was Liza Zanatta Henn, and she said, "we will always remember, we will never forget what the boys of Normandy did." Well, let's help her keep her word. If we forget what we did, we won't know who we are. I'm warning of an eradication of the American memory that could result, ultimately, in an erosion of the American spirit. Let's start with some basics: more attention to American history and a greater emphasis on civic ritual.

And let me offer lesson number one about America: All great change in America begins at the dinner table. So, tomorrow night in the kitchen I hope the talking begins. And children, if your parents haven't been teaching you what it means to be an American, let 'em know and nail 'em on it. That would be a very American thing to do.

And that's about all I have to say tonight, except for one thing. The past few days when I've been at that window upstairs, I've thought a bit of the "shining city upon a hill." The phrase comes from John Winthrop, who wrote it to describe the America he imagined. What he imagined was important because he was an early Pilgrim, an early freedom man. He journeyed here on what today we'd call a little wooden boat; and like the other Pilgrims, he was looking for a home that would be free.

I've spoken of the shining city all my political life, but I don't know if I ever quite communicated what I saw when I said it. But in my mind it was a tall, proud city built on rocks stronger than oceans, wind-swept, God-blessed, and teeming with people of all kinds living in harmony and peace; a city with free ports that hummed with commerce and creativity. And if there had to be city walls, the walls had doors and the doors were open to anyone with the will and the heart to get here. That's how I saw it, and see it still.

And how stands the city on this winter night? More prosperous, more secure, and happier than it was 8 years ago. But more than that: After 200 years, two centuries, she still stands strong and true on the granite ridge, and her glow has held steady no matter what storm. And she's still a beacon, still a magnet for all who must have freedom, for all the pilgrims from all the lost places who are hurtling through the darkness, toward home.

We've done our part. And as I walk off into the city streets, a final word to the men and women across America who for 8 years did the work that brought America back. My friends: We did it. We weren't just marking time. We made a difference. We made the city stronger, we made the city freer, and we left her in good hands. All in all, not bad, not bad at all.

And so, goodbye, God bless you, and God bless the United States of America.

Note: The President spoke at 9:02 p.m. from the Oval Office at the White House. The address was broadcast live on nationwide radio and television.

Ronald Reagan Presidential Library. "Farewell Address to the Nation. (January 11, 1989)" – accessed 8/15/2007

The following article was written by a former U.S. Marine rifle squad leader, W. Thomas Smith, Jr. He writes about military/defense issues and has covered war in the Balkans, on the West Bank, in Iraq and Lebanon. Smith is the author of six books, and his articles appear in a variety of publications, including USA TODAY, National Review Online, Business Week and U.S. News & World Report.

Chapter Thirteen

The Great Christmas Night Raid:
George Washington Leads "America's First Special Operation"

W. Thomas Smith, Jr.

Continental Army General George Washington's celebrated "Crossing of the Delaware" has been dubbed in some military circles, "America's first special operation." Though there were certainly many small-unit actions, raids, and Ranger operations during the Colonial Wars – and there was a special Marine landing in Nassau in the early months of the American Revolution – no special mission by America's first army has been more heralded than that which took place on Christmas night exactly 230 years ago.

Certainly the mission had all the components of a modern special operation (though without all the modern battlefield technologies we take for granted in the 21st century): "A secret expedition" is how John Greenwood, a soldier with the 15th Massachusetts, described it, as quoted in Bruce Chadwick's *The First American Army*.

If nothing else, all the elements for potential disaster were with Washington and his men as they crossed the Delaware River from the icy Pennsylvania shoreline to the equally frozen banks of New Jersey, followed by an eight-mile march to the objective – the town of Trenton.

The river – swollen and swift moving – was full of wide, thick sheets of solid ice. And unlike the romanticized portrayal of the operation in the famous painting by Emanuel Leutze (the one with Washington standing in his dramatic, martial pose; his determined face turned toward the far side of the river), the actual crossing was made in the dead of night, in a gale-like wind and a blinding sleet and snowstorm. Odds are, Washington would have been hunkered down in one of the 66-ft-long wooden boats, draped in his cloak, stoically enduring the bitter cold with his soldiers, some of whom were rowing or poling the boats against the ice and the current.

WASHINGTON'S STRATEGIC CONCERNS

The decision for the crossing and the subsequent raid on Trenton was based on Washington's belief that he had to do something. Otherwise – as he penned in a private letter – "the game will be pretty near up."

To the easily disheartened and the cut-and-runners, it might have seemed "the game" was indeed already "up." After all, many of Washington's Continental Army were wounded, sick, and demoralized. Recent losses to the British had been severe. Desertion numbers were rising, and enlistment terms were almost up. Reinforcements were poorly trained and ill-equipped. Ammunition was in short supply. The soldiers were not properly outfitted for extreme winter conditions: Clothing was spare. Many men were in rags, some "naked," according to Washington's own account. Most had broken shoes or no shoes at all.

THE PLAN

The mission itself, though a huge gamble, was tactically simple.

Washington, personally leading a force of just under 2,500 men, would cross the river undetected, march toward Trenton, and attack the enemy garrisoned in the town at dawn.

Two of Washington's other commanders, Generals John Cadwalader and James Ewing, were also directed to cross: Cadwalader's force was to cross and attack a second garrison near Bordentown. Ewing's force was to cross and block the enemy's escape at Trenton. Both commanders, discouraged by the weather and the river, aborted their own operations. But according to Maurice Matloff's *American Military History* (the U.S. Army's official history), "Driven by Washington's indomitable will, the main force did cross as planned."

Speed of movement, surprise, maneuver, violence of action, and the plan's simplicity were all key. And fortunately, the elements all came together.

The factors in Washington's favor were clear: The weather was so bad that no one believed the Continentals would attempt a river crossing followed by a forced march, much less at night. The Continentals were numerically – and perceived to be qualitatively – inferior to the British Army. The Hessians, mercenaries allied to the British and who were garrisoned in Trenton, had a battlefield reputation that far exceeded their actual combat prowess. And no one believed the weary Americans would want to attempt anything on Christmas.

THE CHRISTMAS

Hours before kickoff, Washington had his officers read to the men excerpts of Thomas Paine's *The American Crisis*, a portion of which reads:

> "These are the times that try men's souls. The summer soldier and the sunshine patriot will, in this crisis, shrink from the service of their country; but he that stands it now, deserves the love and thanks of man and woman. Tyranny, like hell, is not easily conquered; yet we have this consolation with us, that the harder the conflict the more glorious the triumph."

By 4:00 p.m. the force was gathered at McKonkey's Ferry, the launching point for the mission. The watchword, "Victory or death," was given. When darkness set in, the men climbed into the boats and began easing out into the black river.

Back and forth throughout the night and into the wee hours of the 26th, the boat crews ferried the little army, a few horses, and 18 cannons across the Delaware.

The crossing was complete by 4 a.m., but two hours behind schedule, and the temperatures were plummeting. At least two men, exhausted and falling asleep in the snow, froze to death.

ATTACKING TRENTON

The next obstacle was the march toward Trenton in blinding snow, sleet, even hail; and on bloody frostbitten feet. "Keep going men, keep up with your officers," Washington, now on horseback, urged as he rode alongside his advancing infantry.

Just before 8:00 a.m., the advance elements of the American army were spotted on the outskirts of town by a Hessian lieutenant. But by the time he was able to sound the alarm, all hell was breaking loose. Americans were rushing into Trenton with fixed bayonets. The Hessians – some still in their underwear, and nearly all with hangovers from too much Christmas Day celebrating – were attempting to form ranks, but were quickly overrun. Many fled in a panic. Hundreds surrendered. Those who resisted were shot down or run through with the bayonet. The Hessian commander, Col. Johann Rall, was desperately trying to rally his men. But he was shot from his horse, and died later that day.

One of Washington's junior officers, Lieutenant James Monroe was leading a charge against a Hessian position in the town, when he took a musket ball in the chest and collapsed. Amazingly, he survived, and would ultimately become the fifth president of the United States.

The fighting lasted about an hour. Four Americans had been killed and ten-times as many Hessians lay dead in the snow. Some 900 enemy prisoners were rounded up, along with weapons, ammunition, and other desperately needed stores. And Washington's victorious army was soon marching back along the river road to the waiting boats and the return crossing.

WHAT IT MEANT FOR AMERICA

Days later when many enlistments were up, Washington ordered his commanders to form ranks. He then rode out before the troops, and appealed to their sense of duty as well as the critically of their fight:

> "My brave fellows, you have done all I asked
> you to do, and more than could be reasonably
> expected, but your country is at stake… The pre-
> sent is emphatically the crisis which is to decide
> our destiny."

Indeed it was in December of 1776, just as it is in December of 2007.

Washington held his little army together. Many of the continentals renewed their enlistments. They then capitalized on their Trenton victory with wins over the British at Trenton (the second go 'round) on January 2, and Princeton on January 3.

The initial Delaware crossing and the raid on Trenton was the bold, high-risk shot-in-the-arm the nearly disintegrated American army needed in late 1776. The fighting was far from over, and there would be many setbacks for the Americans before the Treaty of Paris was signed formally ending the war in 1783. But the great Christmas night raid in 1776 would forever serve as a model of how a special operation – or a conventional mission, for that matter – might be successfully conducted. There are never any guarantees for success on the battlefield; but with a little initiative and a handful of good Americans, the dynamics of war can be altered in a single night.

Chapter Fourteen

A Patriot's History of The United States

Dr. Larry E. Schweikart

(Excerpt)

Co-Author, Department of History

University of Dayton

A newly-arrived French immigrant unhesitatingly joined the U.S. Army to fight in World War I. His father described the event, writing to Jean-Pierre's sister: "I cannot tell you the mixed sense of joy and pain I have felt . . . without the willingness of all Americans to make these kinds of sacrifices neither the country nor the world would long be free." To me, America means that even the newest citizen represents such a dream, such possibilities, that the nation demands our love and commitment. My family came from the other side in that great conflict, arriving just prior to the outbreak of hostilities in Europe from Germany. Migrating to Arizona, they became farmers, each with the aspirations of a better life for their children, and my father's hard work as a ranch foreman permitted me to be the first of my family to gain a doctorate.

Contrary to the claims of socialists and Marxists, America still represents the "rags to riches" story for millions – but more important, it stands for the possibility of dreams coming true for nearly everyone, at least, those not so embittered by leftist ideology that they refuse to see the forest for the trees. More important still, America still means the freedom to worship as you please, largely without any government interference. More than ever, when God is excluded from civic affairs, it is only the private worship of individuals and churches that will keep America a shining city on a hill.

Chapter Fifteen

"Cheers and Tears"
A Marine's Story of Combat in Vietnam

(Excerpt)
Lt. General Charles G. Cooper
US MARINE CORPS (Retired)

By 1970, the US Air Force had developed very sophisticated night-flying gunships – transport aircraft that could deliver extremely accurate gunfire from a relatively high altitude. The C-130, C-123, and even C-117 aircraft became slow-flying, high-endurance fire bases that used computer-controlled-and-directed fires more accurately than did any other weapon we had in the inventory. The aircraft were especially useful to my battalion because of the large number of small units we had operating independently. There was no other way to give them timely, accurate fire support when they got in trouble. We gave these planes a lot of business.

Our small units were able to talk directly to the pilot or controller in the aircraft. The flight crews would place tracer fire from a variety of guns on a spot, and have the man on the ground adjust their aim. Sometimes these trusty and reliable "birds," some known as "Puff, the Magic Dragon" or "Snuffer Man," would stay on station, giving powerful fire support, for hours, until our unit was in control of the tactical situation. Circling slowly in the dark sky, they would call in additional aircraft when they were getting low on ammunition. I always marveled at the reassuring tone of voice and almost fatherly manner of those aircraft commanders when they were communicating with an excited and badly frightened young Marine. Many were the times I sent a message of praise back to this very special squadron after one of its planes had spent a long, tedious night nursing back into the fold a small Marine unit that had been surrounded by the enemy. I take my hat off to these superb airmen, who still maintain this ability, operating with our nation's special operations forces against America's enemies worldwide.

The variety of skin diseases, foot infections, boils, and intestinal ailments my battalion surgeon dealt with would equate to about 15 years of private practice – as he used to say. Up until late spring, I hadn't been one of his patients, but I had a large boil on my left shoulder that persisted and continued to grow. As we neared the date for an extended field operation, I reached the point where my body armor rubbing on that boil produced unbearable pain. Finally realizing that I had to deal with it, I called Dr. Urban in for a "consultation." I told him of my boil and of our impending raid into the enemy's base area, and asked him to operate on me "tonight." It was thirty minutes before midnight. I did not want to leave the battalion area to go to better facilities: I wanted him to do the necessary surgery in his little sickbay hut. He examined the golf-ball-sized lump and agreed that it needed immediate attention.

Within the hour, the surgeon and his staff performed minor surgery on that damn lump. It was indeed ready for lancing, but a surprise was in store for my young doctor – and for me! As he opened me up and started cleaning the incision, he asked for tweezers. He used them to remove a small silver-colored metal spring, about 1 ½ inches long. He said, "I didn't know you'd been wounded, Colonel. When did this happen?" I told him he was a small child when I was wounded, back in 1951. This was obviously a detonator spring from that Chinese concussion grenade that had blown me down the hill on the 28th of May, 1951. I'd been carrying it around all these years, and it had finally worked its way out. Fortunately, it was accessible. After receiving an antibiotic shot to suppress any infection, I was discharged from sick bay and "returned to duty." It healed "in jig time."

John Curnutt – loyal, efficient, and solid to the end – was to be rotated home in late June. We got a second-tour major, John Sheridan, as his replacement. We started planning for one more major tactical effort before 1/7 was to stand down in late July. I had always wanted to enter the enemy's bread basket, so to speak, in Base Area 112. We made elaborate plans and coordinated them with an operation that the South Vietnamese Marines would be conducting nearby.

Meanwhile, my son Chip had completed his Plebe Year at the Naval Academy. After some initial problems getting his priorities sorted out between Plebe duties and academic duties, he had switched his major and was making excellent grades. During the spring he had written to ask my advice about where he should go on his summer cruise. He could choose a ship in the Atlantic, with an opportunity to visit Europe, or any one of many options in the Pacific, including riding an amphibious ship coming to Danang to start pulling out Marine heavy artillery and engineer equipment. I told him that he should check out the blond-haired, blue-eyed Scandinavians, if at all possible, and leave the war to me. He would have plenty of the Pacific later.

Naturally, he ignored my advice. Late in June I received a post card from Hong Kong saying he was en route to Danang on an LPD. Since I expected to be in the "bush" when he arrived, I asked Colonel Cy Waldrop, who knew Chip from our Camp Lejeune days, to keep an eye out for his ship. I asked him to at least get him off the ship for a meal, if he had the time. I expected to be up to my neck operationally, and didn't think I'd be able to see him when he arrived. He said he'd take care of it.

Two days before we jumped out into BA 112, we found a sizable NVA force moving in daylight about a mile north of LZ Baldy. This was uncharacteristic of the NVA, and we jumped on them with everything we could muster. It almost looked as if they were trying to move into hidden positions near Baldy, possibly for a later attack. At any rate, with the battle joined and two of my companies engaged while the other was being picked by helo, I received a strange message. "Sir, Scatterbox 23 is inbound!"

Scatterbox 23 was the call sign for the commanding general. My God, why does this have to happen when I've found more enemy than we've seen in three months? I asked the operator who was aboard the helo. He checked and said, "Iron Mike's dependent."

I was Iron Mike, so this could only be my son! What was going on? Within a few minutes the helo landed and out jumped Midshipman Third Class

Chip Cooper, wearing Marine utilities, helmet, flak jacket, and a .45 caliber pistol. The helo lifted off, and I waved him over to my bunker. We had received some long-range machine gun fire during the battle that was going on not far from here.

Cy Waldrop had been as good as his word. He had found Chip scrubbing the deck in the crew's head and brought him out to the CG's mess for lunch. As he entered the mess wearing his navy dungarees, General Widdecke saw him. "Aren't you Charlie Cooper's son?" he asked. When Chip said he was, the general said, "Your old man has a small war going on up near LZ Baldy right now. Would you like to go up and see him for about an hour? I'm not going to be using my helo for a while, so you can have a short visit if you'd like. But I can't have you running around in those Navy clothes. Cy, get him in cammies, a flak jacket, helmet, and a pistol. Son, you know how to use a pistol?" Chip said he had fired expert on the .45. And so it came to be. A thoughtful CG, an old friend, and a young son who got to spend about an hour with his old man while he was doing his Marine thing.

We didn't have much private time together, but the battle ended while he was there. I ordered one of the companies nearest Baldy to return through the wire. He joined me as I greeted each of the troops individually as they crossed back inside the perimeter, dirty faced, soaking wet, but smiling as I shook hands with each of them. We had suffered only one minor wound, and the wounded man walked back with this company. Chip, 19 years old at the time, said, "They all look younger than me!" I responded, "That's because they are." He left shortly after that: the general needed his aircraft.

From July 1 to 15 we had worked the eastern portion of the regimental area of operations. On July 16 we were to assault the Song Thu Bon River Valley and the An Chau Dao Mountain Range. We were so far away from friendly artillery that I took my fire base with me – an 81 mm mortar section and a 4-gun platoon of 4.2-inch mortars sited at my command post. The operation was scheduled to last until July 25. I had asked to be relieved of command while in the field, still fighting the enemy on the 24th, rather than upon our return to the rear the next day. Colonel Ed Derning agreed to my request.

It was an ambitious undertaking, but we knew that any operation planned this far in advance had a way of being leaked to the enemy. We maneuvered for three days without any more than occasional contact with small NVA patrols. On the fourth day, I called for two helicopters for a personal air and ground reconnaissance of the river basin. As we were circling the widest point of the river to commence the ground search, I noticed an unusual pattern of gentle mounds on the river banks. They were invisible from the ground, grown over with grass and weeds. We landed next to them, put out local security, and started digging. Mounds indeed! They were dozens of buried warehouses, filled with rice, weapons, ammunition, and assorted medical supplies. Some of these mounds were as long as football fields. After two days of unearthing these huge buried storehouses, we turned the follow-up recovery or destruction of their contents over to the Army Special Forces units that had been operating on the periphery of BA 112.

My closest call of the war came not from the enemy but from ARVN artillery. They had recently been reequipped with Marine 175mm guns. Their airborne spotter aircraft mistook my CP and firebase for an enemy redoubt. Huge shells bracketed us – over, under, left, and right of us. We knew the enemy didn't have these weapons, and the direction suggested they were coming from An Hoa, a joint ARVN/USMC fire base. Using every available means of communication, including airborne observers and screaming voices, we were able to turn off the ARVN cannon cockers before they made one final correction and blew us to smithereens.

The good news was that there were no US casualties and that we discovered much enemy gear. The bad news was that we had no meaningful enemy contact. We did, on this our "graduation exercise," as the troops called it, function perfectly.

There were no speeches at my change of command. Only the CP troops were present, and most of those were out on security duty, but I did bring in one squad from Zulu Company. It was commanded by a six-foot-four black Marine corporal who wore a huge smile on his face. We had been through a lot together. It started at my first request mast and ended, appropriately, with him commanding the one squad of troops in ranks for the brief ceremony. The whole battalion had profited from our relationship. Lieutenant Marye had sent him over to be the "honor guard" as I transferred the battalion colors to Lieutenant Colonel Paul Riegert on July 24, 1970, the day before the battalion was to stand down from field duty.

My war was over. This battalion had become as good as I could make it. Its men were proud and they were good, but my heart still aches when I remember those memorial services.

> *His bayoneted rifle stuck in the ground, his helmet mounted upon it, a Marine has gone to his final place. We who remain behind can only remember, thank God for his friendship, weep, and pray for his loved ones.*

> *From my last memorial service, for Alpha and Bravo Companies in July 1970:*

> *Whenever we lose a true friend, it is natural to ask why, but the answer never comes. Our friendship with these departed comrades has already made our lives better. The true measure of a man's worth in this world is not how long he lived, but the quality of what he left behind. We are the product of the people we associated and served with. These Marines, honored here today, will live in our memories of courage, hardships, and heartaches shared on the field of battle.*

> *They will never be forgotten. I ask God to comfort their families and help them find peace. We who remain thank God for the honor of serving with such brave and selfless men. Amen.*

James C. Dobson, Ph.D., is founder and chairman of Focus on the Family, a non-profit organization that produces his internationally syndicated radio programs, heard on over 3,000 radio facilities in North America and in twenty-seven languages in approximately 4,130 additional facilities in over 160 other countries.

Dr. Dobson has been heavily involved in governmental activities related to the family. He served on the task force which summarized the White House Conference on Families and received a special commendation from President Jimmy Carter in 1980. He was appointed by President Ronald Reagan to the National Advisory Commission to the office of Juvenile Justice and Delinquency Prevention, 1982-84. From 1984-87 he was regularly invited to the White House to consult with President Reagan and his staff on family matters. He served as co-chairman of the Citizens Advisory Panel for Tax Reform, in consultation with President Reagan, and served as a member and later chairman of the United States Army's Family Initiative, 1986-88.

Dr. Dobson is married to Shirley, and he is the father of two grown children, Danae and Ryan. The Dobsons reside in Colorado Springs, Colorado.

Chapter Sixteen

A Memorial Day Message

Dr. James C. Dobson

May 2004

Dear Friends:

In honor of the Memorial Day holiday, I'd like to do something that I don't think I've ever done in this forum. If you'll be so kind as to indulge me, I'm writing this month's letter directly to and about members of the American military, both past, present and future. Those who are serving today are among the finest young men and women our country has produced and they deserve our appreciation, our support, and yes, our prayers too.

Memorial Day affords us an excellent opportunity as Americans to seek ways to honor those special people who represent us in the various branches of the military. This is not only right and proper, but it is the patriotic thing to do. And heaven knows, there has been precious little patriotism seen or heard in this country in recent days. After the horrific tragedies of September 11, 2001, there was a wonderful spirit of unity and oneness that pervaded the land. Do you remember the words "Untied We Stand," and "God Bless America," emblazoned on thousands of billboards and bumper stickers? Whatever happened to that sense of brotherhood, that evident love for God and adoration for our country that prevailed through those troubling days? I fear that era has largely been forgotten, especially in wake of the vitriolic and disturbing presidential campaign that has engulfed the nation.

Our forebears would not have believed the level of hostility that is showing up now in the media. Whether you support President George W. Bush or Senator John Kerry, there should be a certain dignity and respect accorded the office of the Chief Executive and to our other governmental leaders. Instead, an atmosphere of hate has swept into the debate. Last month, a full-page advertisement in a Florida newspaper said the following about Secretary of Defense Donald Rumsfeld: "We should put this [expletive] up against a wall . . . and pull the trigger." I thought advocating the murder of a federal official was against the law, yet no charges have been brought. Billionaire George Soros helped fund a television commercial earlier this year comparing the President with Adolph Hitler. And the *New Republic* recently ran a cover story entitled, "The Case for Bush Hatred." Come on, America. We can do better than that.

Yes, it is time for us to celebrate the full meaning of Memorial Day. Put up American flags in front of your houses. Invite friends to backyard barbecues that feature patriotic themes. And welcome military men and women who are in your communities to join in the festivities. Let them know that we appreciate their willingness to put their lives on the line and make the sacrifices necessary to protect our wonderful nation.

Perhaps we should also take a moment to recall why we pause, collectively and individually, on the last Monday of May, to pay tribute to our fallen heroes. Is it merely the third and final day of a long weekend, or is there more here for all of us to contemplate? Let's review the history of this significant day.

Originally known as "Decoration Day," the holiday was established on May 5, 1868 by the Grand Army of the Republic, an organization of Union veterans. Envisioned as an opportunity for the nation to decorate the graves of the

Civil War dead, General John Login declared May 30 as the official date of commemoration because by that time, flowers would be in bloom all across the country. Ceremonies were first held at Arlington National Cemetery with children from the Soldiers' and Sailors' Orphan Homes placing flowers on both Union and Confederate graves, all the while reciting prayers and singing hymns.

History has a way of sanitizing even the most brutal of circumstances, but can you imagine the pain and sorrow that must have been represented on the green fields of Arlington that first Memorial Day morning? I close my eyes and I can see a little girl of just five or six, a yellow ribbon in her hair, placing a rose beside a granite marker of her father – a man she never knew. He fell at Shiloh, or Antietam, or Vicksburg. I also see a boy of maybe 10, adorned in his Sunday best, who is kneeling in the shadow of a towering oak tree. He is now old enough to read the markings on his dad's grave and mature enough to remember him, too. This is now the final resting place of his father who left with the other idealistic young men who marched off to fight in our nation's bloodiest war. Six hundred thousand of them never came back, and many of those who survived were horribly disfigured and disabled.

The prosperity we share today has been purchased with their blood, sweat and tears, and we cannot, we must not, forget the sacrifices in the Civil War and on a thousand other battlefields around the world. Perhaps we can draw new inspiration from the words of Abraham Lincoln, spoken in a Gettysburg ceremony where so many brave men had recently died. He said,

> The world will little note, nor long remember
> what we say here, but it can never forget what
> they did here. It is for us the living, rather, to be
> dedicated here to the great task remaining before
> us – that from these honored dead we take
> increased devotion to that cause for which they
> gave us the last full measure of devotion – that
> we here highly resolve that these dead shall not

have died in vain – that this nation, under God,
shall have a new birth of freedom – and that government of the people, by the people, for the
people, shall not perish from the earth.

We pray that American military personnel currently deployed in Iraq, Afghanistan and other places around the world will be able to help bring about this "new birth of freedom" of which Lincoln spoke on behalf of those who are oppressed, exploited and imprisoned. We also pray that terrorism will never again be visited upon innocent people in our beloved country.

And now, I welcome you to read along with me as I write a heartfelt letter directly to our women and men in uniform, who are serving in troubled places around the world.

May 2004

I bring warming greetings to you, the American Soldier, Sailor, Marine, Airman and Coast Guardsman:

I speak to you today from our offices in Colorado Springs, Colorado. For over 10 years now, through my westward facing windows, I have been privileged to see some of you soaring in gliders and other small planes, high above the Air Force Academy campus, training for the missions that now put you in harm's way. On a clear day, I can see the famed Cheyenne Mountain, home to the North American Aerospace Defense Command (NORAD).

Further south is situated Fort Carson, home to nearly 20,000 of the bravest fighting men and women on earth. To the east, there is Peterson and Schriever Air Force Base, housing Space Command and numerous other branches of the Armed Forces. What an honor it is to share this small swatch of America with you, though for many, this community has served as temporary quarters en route to various theaters of action. Given the significant military presence in our town, I have seen you in our churches, restaurants, parks and other businesses.

Had I still been in uniform, I would have thrown you the snappiest salute this side of the Mississippi. Yet, as a private citizen now, I want you to know how much we appreciate and love you.

You represent the best this nation has to offer. If only time and circumstance would permit it, I'd love nothing more than to meet each of you individually and tell you how thankful I am for your service and sacrifice.

Wherever you serve, at home or abroad, I offer you my greetings and gratitude this Memorial Day, 2004, on behalf of millions of your countrymen.

Since the dawn of our nation's founding, every generation has endured a time of testing.

From the first skirmish at Lexington, to the burning of the White House in 1812, to Teddy Roosevelt's charge up San Juan Hill, to the carnage and human cost of the Civil War to the death and destruction of World War I to the surprise attacks and subsequent liberations of World War II to the wretched winter campaign of Korea to the stalemate in the jungles of Vietnam and to the more recent war against terrorism and tyranny in the Middle East, this nation has been through the types of trials and conflicts that, as Thomas Paine suggested, "try men's souls."

We are also facing our challenges and dangers this very hour.

The cast of characters may change, but the goal of the enemy has always been the same – to take away the freedoms of others who could not defend themselves.

Last month, in an address to the American people, President Bush summed up the significance behind our tireless fight and the source of our liberties by stating, "Freedom is not this country's gift to the world; freedom is the Almighty's gift to every man and woman in this world."

You might be familiar with a favorite author of mine who writes on issues related to American military history. The late Stephen Ambrose wrote numerous best sellers, ranging from biographies of Presidents Eisenhower and Nixon to various works related to World War II. In *Citizen Soldier*, Mr. Ambrose spoke eloquently to the noble and pure nature of the American warrior.

All throughout history, he said, conquering soldiers looted, raped, pillaged, plundered and even murdered the people they had subdued. Americans in uniform, however, served as a significant exception.

"Everywhere in the world," wrote Ambrose, "whether in Belgium, the Philippines, Germany, or Japan, the sight of a twelve-man squad of GIs brought joy to people's hearts… the sight of those American kids meant cigarettes, candy, C-rations and freedom. They had come, not to conquer, but to liberate."

In reviewing our past military successes, I hope you take great comfort and encouragement in the character of the company you keep.

The Pentagon reports that there are approximately 1.5 million of you spread from one side of the globe to the other, with nearly 135,000 of these same troops currently battling under the hot desert sun of Iraq.

Our media and politicians regularly quote these numbers rather coldly, but I am keenly aware that behind every single number is a name – and a family for whom the name represents an entire world.

Just prior to the attacks of September 11th, I wrote to our constituency regarding the changing face of our military, and thus, the new challenges that accompany these circumstances. Here is what I said in July of 2001:

> Today's military contains many more professionals with specialized skills, many of whom have families. According to the Defense Department, in 1953, only 33 percent of enlisted members were married. When the draft ended in 1973, the figure had risen to 43 percent. Today, 52 percent of active-duty enlisted individuals are married and 71 percent of officers are married. Children are a significant factor, too. Currently, 46 percent of all people on active duty have children.

I went on to acknowledge what you already know: Military life is extremely taxing on families.

Indeed, as many of you came home from the war this past summer, either on leave or as a result of troop rotation, we watched with tear-filled eyes as some of you met newborn babies for the very first time.

Though the cameras captured the joy of reunion, reality suggests that the struggles don't simply end when the soldier arrives safely home.

Money is tight. Patience is thin. A war zone can do cruel things to otherwise happy and adjusted people. Despite the challenges, there is hope to be had.

Over the loudest objections of the ACLU, I urge you to find your strength in the wisdom of the all-wise and all knowing Almighty! This advice doesn't spring forth from the wisdom of my brow, but from the truths of Scripture and the precedent of your comrades who have gone before you.

Hold tightly to the assurances of God, Hear His promise, articulated so eloquently in the 46th Psalm:

"God is our refuge and strength, an ever-present help in trouble. Therefore we will not fear, though the earth give way and the mountains fall into the heart of the sea, though its waters roar and foam and the mountains quake with their surging" (v. 1-3, NIV).

In just a short while, we will remember another incredible day of American sacrifice – D-Day: June 6, 1944. This year marks the 60th anniversary, and I am told our President will preside over what promises to be an emotional ceremony in France. So it has been in days past.

In 1984, on the 40th anniversary of the landing, President Reagan spoke amidst the windswept cliffs of Normandy. His words hold great relevance for both our nation and your efforts today:

> Forty summers have passed since the battle that you fought here. You were young the day you took these cliffs; some of you were hardly more than boys, with the deepest joys of life before you. Yet, you risked everything here. Why? Why did you do it? What impelled you to put aside the instinct for self-preservation and risk your lives to take these cliffs? What inspired all the men of the armies that met here? We look at you, and somehow we know the answer. It was faith and belief. It was loyalty and love.

> The men of Normandy had faith that what they were doing was right, faith that they fought for all humanity, faith that a just God would grant them mercy on this beachhead, or on the next. It was the deep knowledge – and pray God we have

not lost it – that there is a profound moral difference between the use of force for liberation and the use of force for conquest. You were here to liberate, not to conquer, and so you and those others did not doubt your cause. And you were right not to doubt.

You all knew that some things are worth dying for. One's country is worth dying for, and democracy is worth dying for, because it's the most deeply honorable form of government ever devised by man. All of you loved liberty. All of you were willing to fight tyranny, and you knew the people of your countries were behind you.

Something else helped the men of D-Day; their rock-hard belief that Providence would have a great hand in the events that would unfold here; that God was an ally in this great cause. And so, the night before the invasion, when Colonel Wolverton asked his parachute troops to kneel with him in prayer, he told them: Do not bow your heads, but look up so you can see God and ask His blessing in what we're about to do. Also, that night, General Matthew Ridgway on his cot, listening in the darkness for the promise God made to Joshua: 'I will not fail thee nor forsake thee.'

These are the things that impelled them; these are the things that shaped the unity of the Allies. And these are the things that will hold you steady when the world seems to be pulling you apart.

I will leave you with these words: We love you. We are praying for you daily, and you are making us proud in the process.

Your work is not only noble, but it will leave a legacy long after any of us remain here on earth. Please, if you ever find yourself in Colorado Springs, stop by to see us. Every single one of you is an American hero of inestimable worth. May God keep you safe and preserve your families in your absence.

I remain a grateful citizen.

Sincerely,

James C. Dobson, Ph.D. (Founder and Chairman)

<u>Chapter Seventeen</u>

The Flag of the United States of America

Howard Schnauber
The Ft. Collins Public Library Local History Archive

I am the Flag of the United States of America.
My name is Old Glory.
I fly atop the world's tallest buildings.
I stand watch in America's halls of justice.
I fly majestically over great institutes of learning.
I stand guard with the greatest military power in the world.
Look up! And see me!
I stand for peace-honor-truth and justice
I stand for freedom.
I am confident—I am arrogant
I am proud.
When I am flown with my fellow banners
My head is a little higher
My colors a little truer.
I bow to no one.
I am recognized all over the world.
I am worshipped—I am saluted—I m respected
I am revered—I am loved and I am feared.
I have fought every battle of every war for more than 200 years.
Gettysburg, Shiloh, Appomattox, San Juan Hill, the trenches of France,

The Argonne Forest, Anzio, Rome, the beaches of Normandy,
The deserts of Africa, the cane fields of the Philippines, the rice paddies
and jungles of Guam, Okinawa, Japan, Korea, Vietnam, Guadalcanal,
New Britain, Peleliu, and many more islands.
And a score of places long forgotten by all but those who were with me.
I was there.
I led my soldiers—I followed them.
I watched over them.
They loved me
I was on a small hill in Iwo Jima.
I was dirty battle-worn and tired, but my soldiers cheered me,
and I was proud.
I have been soiled, burned, torn and trampled, on the streets of
countries I have helped set free
It does not hurt, for I am invincible.
I have been soiled, burned, torn and trampled on the streets of
my country and when it is by those
with whom I have served in battle—it hurts.
But I shall overcome—for I am strong.
I have slipped the bonds of Earth and stand watch over the
uncharted new frontiers of space
from my vantage point on the moon.
I have been a silent witness to all of America's finest hours,
But my finest hour comes when I am torn into strips to be
used for bandages for my wounded comrades on the field of battle.
When I fly at half mast to honor my soldiers,
And when I lie in the trembling arms of a grieving
mother at the graveside of her fallen son,
I am proud.
My name is Old Glory.
Dear God—long may I wave.

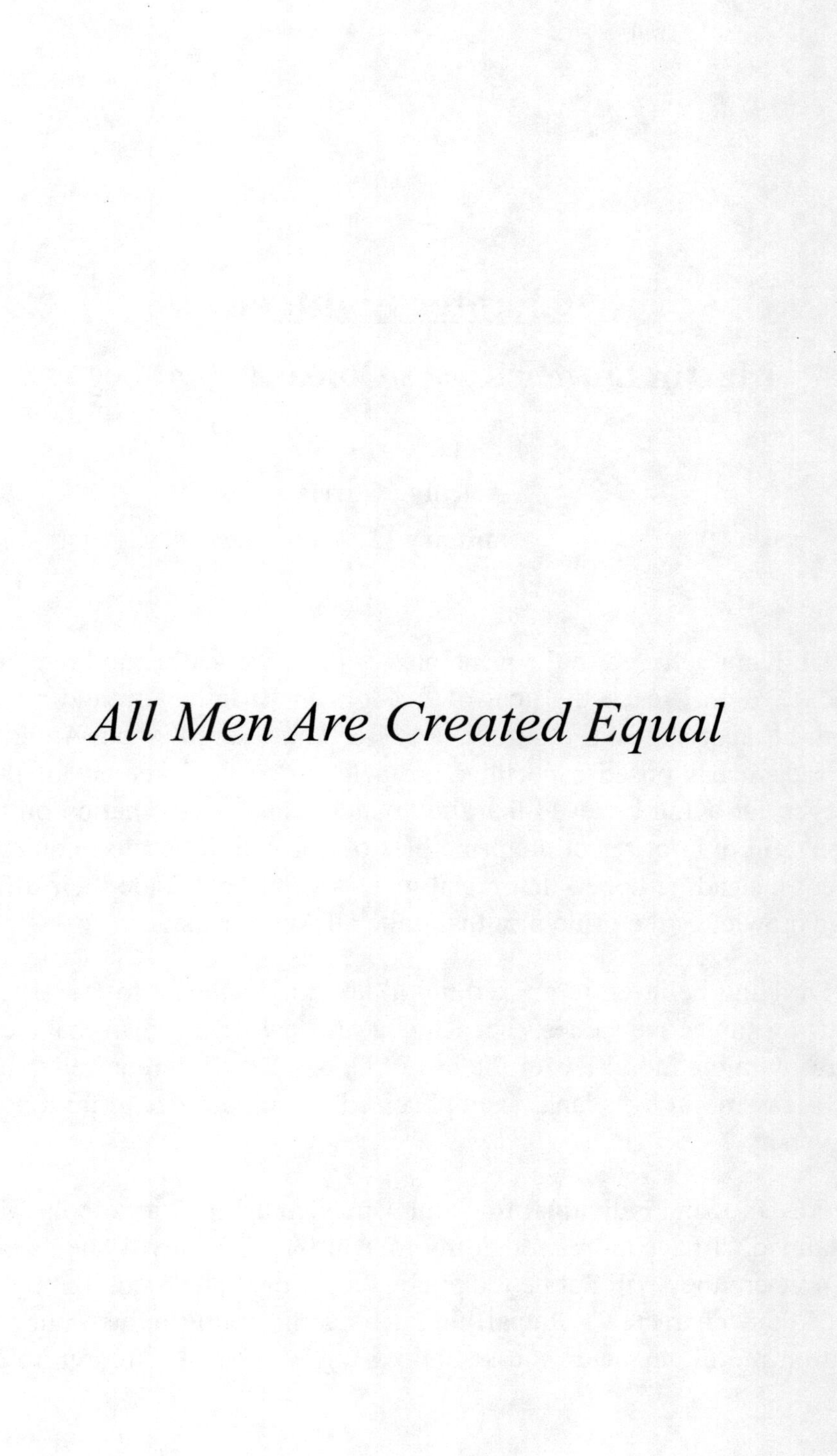

All Men Are Created Equal

Chapter Eighteen

Martin Luther King's Conservative Legacy

(Excerpt)

Carolyn Garris

January 12, 2006

Dr. King believed in the principles of the American Founding. He maintained, "We will reach the goal of freedom in Birmingham and all over the nation, because the goal of America is freedom." Throughout American history, racism has posed a peculiar obstacle to the achievement of that goal. However, Dr. King believed that the Founders had set the nation on the right course. He did not reject the principles of our nation because contradictions existed; instead he hoped that racial groups would put aside their differences and acknowledge the principles that unite all Americans....

Dr. King believed in a fixed moral law, an anathema to moral relativists espousing subjective values. For King, a just law was "a man-made code that squares with the moral law or the law of God." Dr. King required that his followers lead moral lives, and he emphasized the importance of faith in the face of adversity....

For Dr. King, individual freedom depended upon civic responsibility. He proclaimed, "I have a dream that my four little children will one day live in a nation where they will not be judged by the color of their skin but by the content of their character." Racial judgment is inherently unjust, but judgment based on moral character is essential. King wanted his children to live in a colorblind society but not a value-neutral society that rejects all standards of judgment....

In today's parlance, Dr. King's movement would be called "faith-based." Unlike the doggedly secular groups that now campaign for government action in the name of "social justice," King's coalition was explicitly religious, rooted in churches and Christian morality. King's ever-growing congregation labored for reform in Montgomery, in Alabama, and then all across the country. The Montgomery Bus Boycott testifies to the strength of churches and local institutions to make a difference.

<u>Martin Luther King, Jr.</u>

On August 28, 1963, under a nearly cloudless sky, more than 250,000 people, a fifth of them white, gathered near the Lincoln Memorial in Washington to rally for "jobs and freedom." The roster of speakers included people from nearly every segment of society-labor leaders such as Walter Reuther, clergy, film stars including Sidney Poitier and Marlon Brando, and folksingers such as Joan Baez. Each of the speakers was allotted fifteen minutes, but the day belonged to the young and charismatic leader of the Southern Christian Leadership Conference.

Dr. Martin Luther King, Jr. had originally prepared a short and somewhat formal recitation of the sufferings of African Americans attempting to realize their freedom in a society chained by discrimination. He was about to sit down when gospel singer Mahalia Jackson called out, "Tell them about your dream, Martin! Tell them about the dream!" Encouraged by shouts from the audience, King drew upon some of his past talks, and the result became the landmark statement of civil rights in America – a dream of all people, races, colors and backgrounds sharing in an America marked by freedom and democracy.

Chapter Nineteen

"I Have A Dream"

Martin Luther King, Jr.
(August 28, 1963)

I am happy to join with you today in what will go down in history as the greatest demonstration for freedom in the history of our nation.

Five score years ago, a great American, in whose symbolic shadow we stand today, signed the Emancipation Proclamation. This momentous decree came as a great beacon light of hope to millions of Negro slaves who had been seared in the flames of withering injustice. It came as a joyous daybreak to end the long night of their captivity.

But 100 years later, the Negro still is not free. One hundred years later, the life of the Negro is still sadly crippled by the manacles of segregation and the chains of discrimination. One hundred years later, the Negro lives on a lonely island of poverty in the midst of a vast ocean of material prosperity. One hundred years later, the Negro is still languishing in the corners of American society and finds himself an exile in his own land. So we have come here today to dramatize a shameful condition.

In a sense we've come to our nation's capital to cash a check. When the architects of our republic wrote the magnificent words of the Constitution and the Declaration of Independence, they were signing a promissory note to which every American was to fall heir. This note was a promise that all men, yes, black men as well as white men, would be guaranteed the unalienable rights of life, liberty, and the pursuit of happiness.

It is obvious today that America has defaulted on this promissory note insofar as her citizens of color are concerned. Instead of honoring this sacred obligation, America has given the Negro people a bad check, a check which has come back marked "insufficient funds."

But we refuse to believe that the bank of justice is bankrupt. We refuse to believe that there are insufficient funds in the great vaults of opportunity of this nation. So we have come to cash this check — a check that will give us upon demand the riches of freedom and the security of justice. We have also come to this hallowed spot to remind America of the fierce urgency of now. This is no time to engage in the luxury of cooling off or to take the tranquilizing drug of gradualism. Now is the time to make real the promises of democracy. Now is the time to rise from the dark and desolate valley of segregation to the sunlit path of racial justice. Now is the time to lift our nation from the quick sands of racial injustice to the solid rock of brotherhood. Now is the time to make justice a reality for all of God's children.

It would be fatal for the nation to overlook the urgency of the moment. This sweltering summer of the Negro's legitimate discontent will not pass until there is an invigorating autumn of freedom and equality. Nineteen sixty-three is not an end, but a beginning. Those who hope that the Negro needed to blow off steam and will now be content will have a rude awakening if the nation returns to business as usual. There will be neither rest nor tranquility in America until the Negro is granted his citizenship rights. The whirlwinds of revolt will continue to shake the foundations of our nation until the bright day of justice emerges.

But there is something that I must say to my people who stand on the warm threshold which leads into the palace of justice. In the process of gaining our rightful place we must not be guilty of wrongful deeds. Let us not seek to satisfy our thirst for freedom by drinking from the cup of bitterness and hatred.

We must forever conduct our struggle on the high plane of dignity and discipline. We must not allow our creative protest to degenerate into physical violence. Again and again we must rise to the majestic heights of meeting physical force with soul force. The marvelous new militancy which has engulfed the Negro community must not lead us to a distrust of all white people, for many of our white brothers, as evidenced by their presence here today, have come to realize that their destiny is tied up with our destiny. They have come to realize that their freedom is inextricably bound to our freedom. We cannot walk alone.

And as we walk, we must make the pledge that we shall always march ahead. We cannot turn back. There are those who are asking the devotees of civil rights, "When will you be satisfied?" We can never be satisfied as long as the Negro is the victim of the unspeakable horrors of police brutality. We can never be satisfied, as long as our bodies, heavy with the fatigue of travel, cannot gain lodging in the motels of the highways and the hotels of the cities. We cannot be satisfied as long as the Negro's basic mobility is from a smaller ghetto to a larger one. We can never be satisfied as long as our children are stripped of their selfhood and robbed of their dignity by signs stating "For Whites Only." We cannot be satisfied as long as a Negro in Mississippi cannot vote and a Negro in New York believes he has nothing for which to vote. No, no, we are not satisfied, and we will not be satisfied until justice rolls down like waters and righteousness like a mighty stream.

I am not unmindful that some of you have come here out of great trials and tribulations. Some of you have come fresh from narrow jail cells. Some of you have come from areas where your quest for freedom left you battered by the storms of persecution and staggered by the winds of police brutality. You have been the veterans of creative suffering. Continue to work with the faith that unearned suffering is redemptive.

Go back to Mississippi, go back to Alabama, go back to South Carolina, go back to Georgia, go back to Louisiana, go back to the slums and ghettos of our northern cities, knowing that somehow this situation can and will be changed.

Let us not wallow in the valley of despair. I say to you today, my friends - so even though we face the difficulties of today and tomorrow, I still have a dream. It is a dream deeply rooted in the American dream.

I have a dream that one day this nation will rise up and live out the true meaning of its creed: "We hold these truths to be self-evident: that all men are created equal."

I have a dream that one day on the red hills of Georgia the sons of former slaves and the sons of former slave owners will be able to sit down together at the table of brotherhood.

I have a dream that one day even the state of Mississippi, a state sweltering with the heat of injustice, sweltering with the heat of oppression, will be transformed into an oasis of freedom and justice.

I have a dream that my four little children will one day live in a nation where they will not be judged by the color of their skin but by the content of their character.

I have a dream today.

I have a dream that one day, down in Alabama, with its vicious racists, with its governor having his lips dripping with the words of interposition and nullification; one day right there in Alabama, little black boys and black girls will be able to join hands with little white boys and white girls as sisters and brothers.

I have a dream today.

I have a dream that one day every valley shall be exalted, every hill and mountain shall be made low, the rough places will be made plain, and the crooked places will be made straight, and the glory of the Lord shall be revealed, and all flesh shall see it together.

This is our hope. This is the faith that I go back to the South with. With this faith we will be able to hew out of the mountain of despair a stone of hope. With this faith we will be able to transform the jangling discords of our nation into a beautiful symphony of brotherhood. With this faith we will be able to work together, to pray together, to struggle together, to go to jail together, to stand up for freedom together, knowing that we will be free one day.

This will be the day when all of God's children will be able to sing with a new meaning, "My country, 'tis of thee, sweet land of liberty, of thee I sing. Land where my fathers died, land of the pilgrim's pride, from every mountain-side, let freedom ring."

And if America is to be a great nation this must become true. So let freedom ring from the prodigious hilltops of New Hampshire. Let freedom ring from the mighty mountains of New York. Let freedom ring from the heightening Alleghenies of Pennsylvania.

Let freedom ring from the snowcapped Rockies of Colorado. Let freedom ring from the curvaceous slopes of California.

But not only that; let freedom ring from Stone Mountain of Georgia.

Let freedom ring from Lookout Mountain of Tennessee.

Let freedom ring from every hill and molehill of Mississippi - from every mountainside.

Let freedom ring. And when this happens, when we allow freedom to ring, when we let it ring from every village and every hamlet, from every state and every city, we will be able to speed up that day when all of God's children, black men and white men, Jews and Gentiles, Protestants and Catholics, will be able to join hands and sing in the words of the old Negro spiritual, "Free at last! Free at last! Thank God Almighty, we are free at last!"

Chapter Twenty

Remember 9/11

Dr. Herbert London

From the building I reside in, I can see the World Trade Center (WTC) site, where a hole in the ground is a constant reminder of the 9/11 terrorist attacks on the United States. But in the area surrounding the WTC site, what we local residents call "our hole," there is extraordinary development.

The Goldman Sachs building is going up across the street. A supermarket is being built two blocks away. High-rise buildings seem to rise magically, as if defying construction requirements. Battery Park, where there are sweeping views of the Statue of Liberty and Ellis Island, has been refurbished with a magnificent fountain and new gardens. A dramatic tunnel is under construc-tion, connecting the subway system to the Staten Island ferry terminal.

Despite "our hole," downtown New York is alive, prospering, and electric with possibilities. In many essential ways this description is a metaphor for the United States five years after the 9/11 attacks.

Our country has been scarred but remains resilient. The attack has clearly affected American attitudes. People are wary about unidentified packages in the subway system, and September 11 continues to be a day of remembrance and sadness. However, the dynamism that characterizes the United States is undiminished.

As I stood on Church Street staring at the WTC site last September 11, five tourists asked if I would join them for a spontaneous rendition of "God Bless America." My wife and I sang as tears rolled down our cheeks. We were united with strangers who wished to recall what America stands for. We were sad but steadfast; united in our appreciation of America and determined to resist those who would destroy our way of life.

To some degree, 9/11 has faded from our collective memory. Patriotic sentiment is recalled, as my experience would suggest, but it has lost its immediacy. What is most noteworthy is that the spirit of America remains intact.

William Tyler Page wrote in *American Creed*, "I . . . believe it is my duty to my country to love it, support its Constitution, to obey its law, to respect its flag, and to defend it against all enemies." Surely there are many in this land of the free who have the constitutional right to disagree, but, in my opinion, the overwhelming majority of Americans embrace this sentiment. Pegged into this position are words such as love, honor, loyalty, pride, devotion, and sacrifice, words that suggest an emotional attachment. But patriotism for most Americans is not only reflexive emotion; it is also reasoned argument.

Alexis de Tocqueville in *Democracy in America* claimed that customs, traditions, and a reverence for the past are emphasized, but that patriotism for Americans is a state of mind in which "citizens . . . grapple with the various aspects of America which are not so rose-colored."

As I see it, 9/11 has brought to the fore liberal patriots who believe that they must work for political change consistent with their interpretation of the national creed and conservative patriots who maintain an allegiance to the nation based on what the Founding Fathers intended. The differences are textured, representing perspective rather than the basic concepts, which remain largely undisturbed.

September 11, 2001, was a fateful day for the nation, yet remarkably the notion of "my country, right or wrong" has not gained a foothold. Americans may be justifiably angry about those who would attack our land and people, but we are perpetually self-critical, as any viewing of television news would suggest. We also have a well-ensconced memory of the good and a faith in our ability to change when that is necessary.

Hence my recollection of the horror of five years ago evokes a belief in human possibility and the stirring example of Americans who pick themselves up, dust themselves off, and look to shape the days ahead.

Jacques Maritain once noted that what set the United States apart from other nations is that it is in "a continual state of becoming." The destruction the nation endured has forced Americans to look in the mirror to see strengths and warts, to regard the remarkable achievements and the challenges over the horizon.

There are, of course, those who embody the "historical grievance" position. What they see are only flaws. In each overheated claim they make, there is an incremental decline in the spirit that sustains patriotism. After all, why should anyone care about a nation of colonizers and imperialists, words that have been transmogrified into crimes?

Five years of reflection after the 9/11 attacks have refurbished Americans' belief in their country. In the end, even reasoned patriots who carefully weigh errors, mistakes, tragedy, and accomplishment will find something positive on which to hang patriotic sentiment.

That hole in the ground sits as a reminder of human frailty and imperfectability, but it has not sapped a belief in ourselves or the will for regeneration.

There is a park soon to be completed where the World Trade Center once stood majestically. Several days ago I walked on this newly constructed path, and in the shadow of the Twin Towers that remains embedded in my mind, I noticed a row of seedlings about to blossom.

Five years ago there was only dust on that ground, now flowers are about to bloom. Here is the United States five years after 9/11: In the midst of despoliation, life appears doggedly fighting for a place in the sun.

Chapter Twenty-One

In Loving Memory of the Victims of the Terrorist Attacks on Sept. 11, 2001

Albert F. Chestone

"IF ONLY TEARS AND MEMORIES
COULD BUILD
A STAIRWAY TO HEAVEN"

Our heaven-aimed twin towers have been destroyed,
Our beautifully designed Pentagon was set afire.
A terrorist's hijacked plane crashed in an open field in Shanksville, PA,
This was their goal, this was their ultimate desire.
They collaborated, trained and studied,
To execute their plan.
Determined to draw attention,
To their Godless beliefs, upon which they stand.
They are despicable cowards, and murderers,
Nestled in a satanic cell
Whose worthiness the Lord will one day judge,
Whether to enter His Kingdom, or be cast into a fiery Hell.
They have crumbled our pillared towers,
Crashed-landed one of our planes and purposely damaged our Pentagon,
But our freedom still rings loud and clear,
And our God-given "American Spirit" will forever live on.
Yet we ask, "why did innocent people have to die?"

As we are tormented with memories and unashamedly cry.
Our President spoke and he touched the hearts of our great nation,
And shared a promise, of a carefully planned, destructive retaliation.
The response of volunteers to the scene of the crime,
Gave evidence of a loving, brotherly sign.
Neither race, creed nor color, mattered at all,
As caring Americans, we stood erect, proud, strong and ever so tall.
Firemen, medical personnel and people of all trades and professions,
Forged and linked a chain of unity,
As dedicated law enforcement officials successfully pieced together
The terrorist puzzle, without regard for impunity.
Farewell, our beloved brothers and sisters,
As you take comfort in the Lord's warm embrace,
We will pause often for the rest of our lives and search our hearts,
Reflecting on how each of you touched the whole human race.
We thank God for our freedom, our spirit and our spacious skies,
The fruited plain and the amber waves of grain.
But most of all, we treasured your life with us,
And now you are with the Lord, in whom our country has its greatest trust.

(My loving wish is expressed in these beautiful words of an unknown author)

"If only tears could build a stairway,
and memories a lane,
we would all walk to Heaven,
and bring you home again."

Chapter Twenty-Two

Character – Courage – Community

Vincent J. Bove, CPP
Renown Public Speaker
Short Hills, New Jersey

As a leadership and security educator dedicated to the transforming of America through a renewal of our proud heritage of character, courage and community, America is all about the service of others.

Recently, I was humbled with the reception of the FBI Director's Award for Community Leadership for my work in combating crime, terrorism, drugs and violence in America. In receiving this award, I share these remarks which succinctly summarizes my thoughts on America as exemplified through so many who serve their communities, families, agencies and nation:

It is an honor to receive the FBI Director's Community Leadership award but it is also very humbling. There are so many individuals deserving of recognition and I would like to share this award with those I have recently met from throughout the nation.

Victims and Families of the Virginia Tech Tragedy

These families experienced the worst act of school violence in our nation's history. In my communications with many of them since the April 16 tragedy, I have found them to represent the Courage of America.

Future Leaders of America

Just last week at the National Conference on Ethics in America at the United States Military Academy at West Point, I was privileged to serve college students from throughout the nation. These students of character assembled to exchange concerns and solutions for restoring the moral compass of our nation and represent the Hope of America.

Members of the INEOA

As a privileged speaker during the recent International Narcotics Officers Association's annual conference, I had the opportunity to interact with individuals representing local law enforcement as well as FBI, DEA and ICE. They clearly represent the Dedication of America.

Members of the FBI

Each of you, in all of the different roles within the FBI, are deserving of respect for the safeguarding of our nation and represent the Commitment of America.

Members of our Armed Forces

At the end of each of my presentations, I always take a few moments to honor those in our military who represent the Service of America.

After one of these services, Marion Dooley, whose on Mark was killed in action while serving in Iraq, thanked me for remembering our soldiers and invited me to attend his military interment ceremony at Arlington National Cemetery. In Arlington, she shared with me a letter given to her by her son Mark which was only to be opened upon his death. Encouraged by Mrs. Dooley, I shared this letter in a recent article since it represents the Honor of America.

I dedicate this award

- to each of you gathered here today,

- to our military personnel, especially Lt. Mark Dooley, and his family,

- to the students from the National Conference on Ethics in America and students and teachers throughout the nation,

- to the members of the INEOA and all those in law enforcement, and

- to all of the victims and families of the Virginia Tech tragedy and other incidents of school violence.

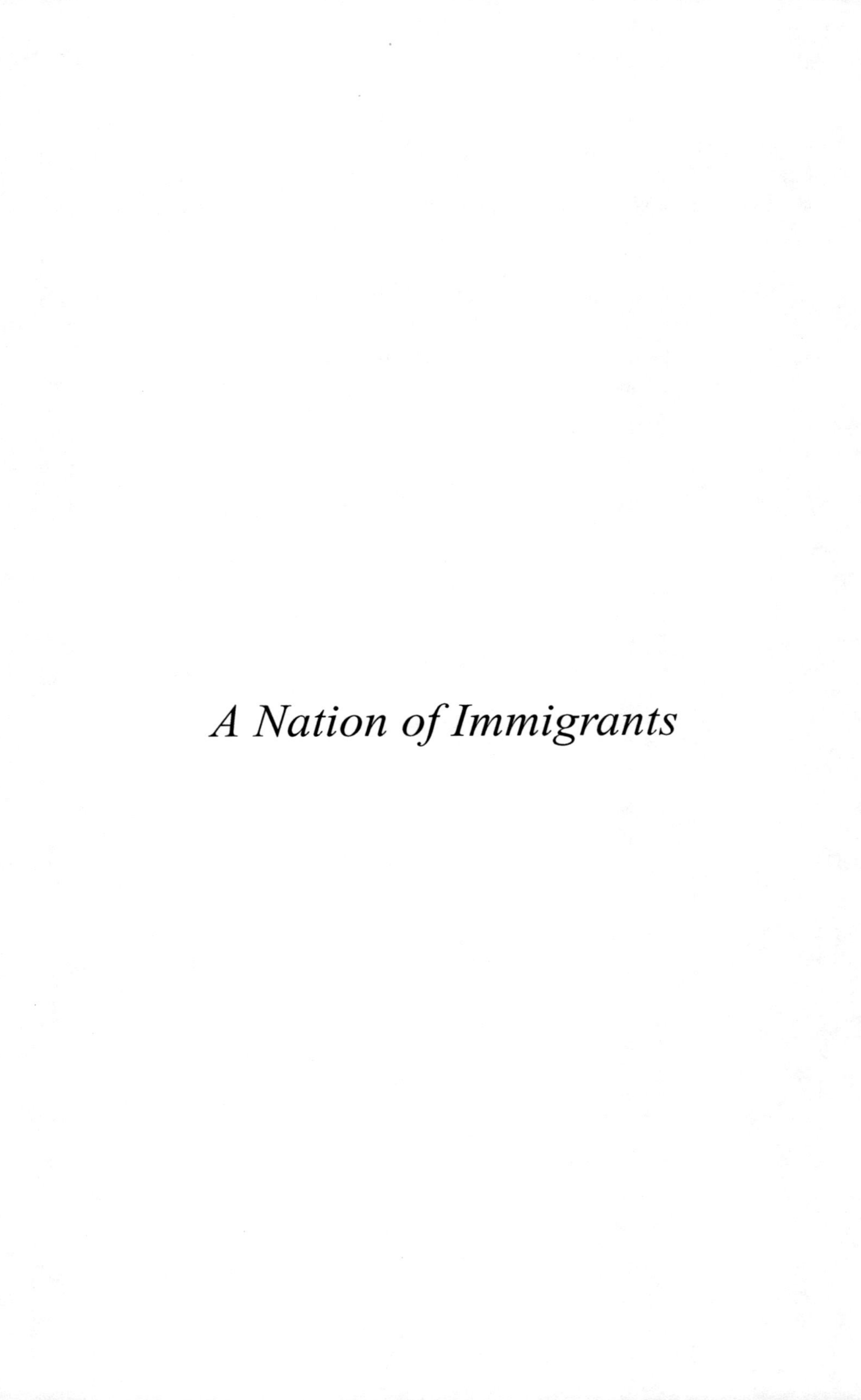

A Nation of Immigrants

Ideas On Immigration

In 1907, Theodore Roosevelt said:

> "In the first place, we should insist that if the immigrant who comes here in good faith becomes an American and assimilates himself to us, he shall be treated on an exact equality with everyone else, for it is an outrage to discriminate against any such man because of creed, or birthplace, or origin. But this is predicated upon the person's becoming in every facet an American, and nothing but an American… There can be no divided allegiance here. Any man who says he is an American, but something else also, isn't an American at all. We have room for but one flag, the American flag… We have room for but one language here, and that is the English language… and we have room for but one sole loyalty and that is a loyalty to the American people."

Chapter Twenty-Three
Addressing Illegal Immigration

Robert Cox
Williamsburg, Virginia

I have moved from frustrated to angry over our elected representatives' unwillingness to address the very consequential problem of illegal immigration. Among the most important responsibilities of government are protecting the citizenry from physical harm, maintaining social order and creating an economic environment in which individuals have a reasonable opportunity to prosper. The failure of our government to deal with illegal immigration has negative implications for each of these responsibilities. Porous borders clearly expose us to the unacceptable threat that terrorists can too easily enter our country and wreak havoc. The multitudes of illegal immigrants that cross our borders each year can, if allowed to continue, destabilize social order because of the inability to assimilate so many people (some of whom are serious criminals), especially if they must stay outside the customary systems and don't have a fundamental desire to adapt to "American values and way of life." The implications of illegal immigration on our economy are both complex and substantial. The drain on public budgets for education, health care, incarceration and welfare systems is enormous, especially in states proximate to our southern border.

What should we do? My plea to our elected officials is that they look at the issue broadly at a policy level. First, consider how many immigrants we need to sustain our economy to make up for the fact that our current birthrate will not generate enough workers to maintain the level of economic growth we desire and are accustomed to, even after considering increased productivity.

Next, assess what sorts of skills will be needed to fuel that economic growth. Education must play a substantial role in this determination. Finally, give consideration to achieving a reasonable geographic dispersion among the immigrants. Of course, political asylum and other special cases should continue to be a part of our immigration system, within reason. After these determinations are made, immigration laws and quotas should be appropriately modified. In short, we should decide who we should allow into our country, establish a manageable process of admitting them, and assertively prevent all others from gaining illegal entry. Otherwise, our economy, social stability and physical security will increasingly be at risk because we don't limit immigration to a level we can reasonably absorb, and have no idea of who is entering our country, for what purpose, and their aggregate effect.

Chapter Twenty-Four

Our Rich Treasure… Our Immigrants

By: Albert F. Chestone

Rarely, if ever, does anyone defect from the United States of America, for we are a proud nation made up of immigrants from every corner of the world. Therefore we are a nation that welcomes the cultures of all immigrants, who settle in this great nation. We are a nation that encourages the free and voluntary cultural celebrations of all ethnic groups, who are proud to do so. While we enjoy such proud moments of celebration, we also know wihin our hearts we believe – whether native born or naturalized – in the words of our Pledge of Allegiance to America. We believe all that America stands for—our own culture, humanity, heritage, flag, Pledge of Allegiance, English language and our own form of government.

As Americans, we take great pride in our country and we do indeed welcome with open arms, all legal immigrants from all nations of the world. Those of us who were fortunate to have been born in America are aware that we possess proud immigrant lineage. This special pride has and continues to reinforce our love for America, its willing to obey the laws of the land, so that we can live in peace and harmony with one another.

These then, are the basic traits that make up a true and patriotic American. If you are a new legal arrival in our beautiful country, awaiting a particular assigned status and eventual citizenship, we would expect that you will most willingly endeavor to adjust as native Americans do by adapting to our culture, our heritage, our history, our humanity, our laws, with the fervent and determined desire to learn, and gradually understand and speak our English language and to make English your primary language. All of these expectations should be naturally understood and embraced. I truly believe that most, if not all legal immigrants from all over the world, who settle in the United States, will view favorably the following comments as set forth, mindful that as accepted immigrants, they have agreed to follow and obey the rules governing legal immigration and have expressed their belief in our form of government.

Shortly after 9/11, somewhat similar articles about immigrants were written by an anonymous American citizen, as well as an anonymous nun. The American citizen made reference to the fact that the dust from the terrorist attacks of 9/11 had barely settled when the politically correct crowd began complaining that our patriotism was offending others.

This person further wrote:

> I am not against immigration, nor do I hold a grudge against anyone who is seeking a better life by coming to America. Our population is almost entirely made up of descendants of immigrants. However, there are a few things that those who have recently come to our country, and apparently some born here, need to understand. This idea of America being a multicultural community has served only to dilute our sovereignty and our national identity. As Americans, we have our own culture, our own society, our own language and our own lifestyle. This culture has been developed over centuries of struggles, trials and victories by millions of men and women, who have sought freedom.

What follows are some excerpts from a similar article written by an anonymous nun who said:

> Our forefathers fought, bled and died at places such as Bunker Hill, Antietam, San Juan, Iwo Jima, Normandy, Korea, and Vietnam. We speak

English, not Spanish, Arabic, Chinese, Japanese, Russian, or any other language. Therefore, if you wish to become part of our society, learn our language.

"In God We Trust" is our national motto. This is not some off-the-wall, Christian, right-wing political slogan on our currency. It is engraved in stone in the House of Representatives, in our Capitol and it is printed on our currency. We adopted this motto because Christian men and women founded this nation on Christian principles, and this is clearly documented throughout our history. If it is appropriate for our motto to be inscribed in the halls of our highest level of government, then it is certainly appropriate to display it on the walls of our schools. God is in our pledge, our National Anthem, nearly every patriotic song and in our founding documents. We honor His birth, death and resurrection as holidays, and we turn to Him in prayer in times of crisis. …

We celebrate Independence Day, Memorial Day, Veterans Day, and Flag Day. We have parades, picnics and barbecues where we proudly wave our flag. As an American, I have the right to wave my flag, sing my national anthem, quote my national motto and cite my pledge whenever and wherever I choose. …

In America, you take your right to complain for granted. The more patriotism that is removed from where our children are taught, the less our children will learn about what it is to be an American and our nation's spirit will slowly be killed. Keep patriotism alive.

To have been born or legally immigrated to the United States or to other free democracies is indeed an honor and a privilege. Unfortunately, there are times when some individuals tend to forget this honor, this privilege, and this freedom, by committing criminal or terrorist acts, or to undertake subversive action to destroy peaceful democracies. Such individuals must be made to understand that the freedom they enjoy within a democratic nation should be regarded as a treasure.

It is the greatness of America and all that it represents, that enables me to proudly say that this is "What America Means To Me."

Mr. Mauro E. Mujica is the Chairman of the Board of U.S. English, Inc., and Rob Toonkel is the Director of Communications.

U.S. English, Inc., the nation's largest non-partisan, non-profit citizens' action group, is dedicated to preserving the unifying role of a common language in America. It was established by the Honorable S.I. Hayakawa, noted educator and former U.S. Senator from California and himself an immigrant to the United States.

Chapter Twenty-Five

A Letter from the Chairman

Mauro E. Mujica
Chairman of the Board
(U.S. ENGLISH)

Dear Fellow Americans,

The single most important element of a strong, unified nation is a common language for all people. Our common language, English, has helped to make the United States the lone superpower in the world today. Our economic system and the guaranteed freedoms we enjoy are the envy of the entire world.

More than 40 years ago, I came from Chile to study architecture at Columbia University. Five years after my arrival I was very proud to become a United States citizen. I know firsthand why it is so important for all the people of our country to understand English. I also know at the deepest personal level, that it is impossible for the new immigrants who are arriving on our shores daily to ever be fully participating members of our society – and take advantage of our unparalleled economic opportunities – unless they learn to use English.

I've been fortunate enough to have done a great deal of business and personal travel throughout the world. I have seen many countries beset with the political problems that result from division and disunity. I can think of no more destructive, even anarchic, situation than losing the common bond that unites all Americans – English.

Since accepting my position of leadership at U.S. ENGLISH in 1993, I feel more strongly than ever about the absolute need to preserve our nation's basic unity. Bureaucrats, politicians, and special interest groups are promoting a multilingual government that is taking away the incentive to learn English. Such misguided policies will result in a linguistically segregated society, leading us to be the Divided States of America.

Your support for U.S. ENGLISH will guarantee that the unity and opportunity that is afforded by one common language will be available to future generations calling America their home.

Chapter Twenty-Six

English Our Greatest Unifier
By: Robert D. Toonkel

Rob Toonkel

English, our common language, has been the greatest unifier of the United States for more than 200 years. it is a symbol of being American, ranking equally with the flag, the bald eagle and the "Star Spangled Banner."
Having English as our official language is a win-win situation for everyone. Through the government establishment of a common language policy, we will encourage and assist newcomers in learning English, knocking down language barriers that keep many from success. Promoting English will allow everyone – no matter their native tongue – to communicate with each other, sharing more of the ideas and cultures that make our nation great. And, it will save the country millions of dollars that would otherwise be spent on unnecessary translation services while providing for common sense exceptions in areas of public safety, health care and tourism.

In this age of diversity, we need a cultural glue to cement our unity as citizens and residents of the same land. Only through a common language can we ensure that all Americans, newcomers and natives alike, can participate in government and go wherever their dreams may take them. In the words of California Senator and U.S. English founder S.I. Hayakawa, "Bilingualism for the individual is fine, but not for a country." For the benefit of Americans, it is time to make this vision a reality.

In a speech introducing official English legislation in the 97th Congress, Senator S.I. Hayakawa began by telling his colleagues, "Language is a unifying instrument which binds people together. When people speak one language they become as one, they become a society."

In the United States, there are more than 300 languages spoken by the 300 million people that call the 50 states home. Instead of standing divided by our many differences, Americans stand unified because of our one common trait – the ability to communicate in English, our common language. Few other assets have the power to bring such diversity together.

English is more than a language in the United States. It is the ticket to financial success. It is the sail through an ocean of career challenges, ranging from a simple job interview to the SAT, LSAT and MCAT, just to name a few. It is the channel through which the immigrant from Mexico can share Mexican Independence Day with the immigrant from China who celebrates the Chinese New Year. It is how we share our cultures and dreams, but most important, it is what unites us as Americans.

In a world where borders continue to dissolve, we should always expand our knowledge of world cultures and world languages. Yet as global leaders call upon their citizens to learn English, and the research linking Americans' knowledge of English to increased income and better health continues to grow, the lesson is clear. For a brighter today and a better tomorrow, the official language should be English, now more than ever.

> By emphasizing the importance of a common language, we safeguard a proud legacy and help to ensure that America's future will be as great as her past.

President Ronald Reagan

> If we are one people not by virtue of common blood, or race, or origin. We are one people, above all, because we hold certain truths to be self-evident; among thee are the truths that all men are created equal, and that just government

is by consent of the government. And government by consent means government by discussion, by debate, by discourse, by argument. Such a common enterprise requires a common language.

— William J. Bennett

Conclusion

U.S. English Foundation, Inc.

There is little doubt that this overwhelming desire for English is based upon the knowledge that in most non-English speaking nations. English fluency permits far greater job opportunities and far higher incomes than fluency in the native language alone. For many nations of the world, English may be the second language learned, but it is the first language in determining economic power.

language of economic power, it is the language of education, communication and in many cases, economic survival. To begin climbing the ladder of success, Americans must have the ability to converse in English, regardless of their ability to speak another language. While we should continue to push for additional foreign language learning opportunities in the United States, we should not let our vision be clouded by gazing at the wrong indicator.

Americans may be more monolingual than we'd desire, but so long as they are monolingual in English, we will be able to ensure that our citizens are ready for educational and employment opportunities in the Untied States. fluent in English.

In this connection, Theodore Roosevelt said, "Every immigrant who comes here should be required within five years to learn English or leave the country."

The Challenges of Freedom

Chapter Twenty-Seven
Why the Pledge of Allegiance Matters

Senator Tom McClintock
of California

There is a reason behind the movement to strike the words "under God" from the Pledge of Allegiance – and from our national customs, and our currency, and our public ceremonies. It has very little to do with atheism. It has a great deal to do with authoritarianism.

The philosophy of the American Founding is unique among the nations of the world because of a bedrock principle that was given expression with words in the Declaration of Independence that are old and familiar, and yet not often pondered these days.

In the American view, there is a certain group of rights that are accorded absolutely and equally to every individual and that cannot be alienated by others. The existence of these rights is beyond debate – "self-evident" in the words of the Founders. And their source is supreme – "the Creator."

"We hold these truths to be self-evident, that all men are created equal, that they are endowed by their Creator with certain unalienable rights…"

What are these rights? They are rights that exist as a condition of human life itself. If an individual were alone in the world, the rights he has are those rights the Founders traced to "the laws of Nature and of Nature's God." In their words, "…that among these are life, liberty, and the pursuit of happiness." The right to the fruit of our own labor, the right to express our own sentiments, the right to defend ourselves, the right to live our lives according to our own best lights – in a word, Freedom.

But how do we secure these rights in a world where others seek to violate them? We form a government servient to these God-given rights – or more precisely, a government under God. "That to secure these rights, governments are instituted among men…" In the American view, the only legitimate exercise of force by one individual over another, or by a government over its people, is in the defense of these natural rights.

This concept is the foundation of American liberty. And because it defines limits to the powers of government, it is supremely offensive to the radicals of the Left. They abhor the words "under God" because these words "under God" stand in the way of an all-powerful state.

The French and American revolutions were waged on precisely the same declared rights of liberty and equality. One was a ghastly failure that ended in the Reign of Terror; the other, a magnificent success. Why?

In the philosophy of the French Revolution, the rights of man were defined by a governmental committee and extended at the sufferance of that government. In the American view, these rights come from God, their existence is pre-eminent and their preservation is the principal object of government.

If the source of our fundamental rights is not God, then the source that becomes man – or more precisely, a government of men. And rights that can be extended by government may also be withdrawn by government.

Words matter. Ideas matter. And symbols matter. The public furor fomented by the Ninth Circuit Court over the Pledge of Allegiance must not be devalued as a mere defense of harmless deistic references and quaint old customs. The principle at stake is central to the very foundation of the American nation and the very survival of its freedoms.

Chapter Twenty-Eight

America:
Making Real the Promise of Hope

(Excerpt)

Dr. Paula Franzese

As a young attorney and new law professor, I remember phoning home, and speaking with my dad. My dad was an immigrant, never formally educated but committed deeply to the power and promise of knowledge. He was very wise. I had been working on a pro bono housing court reform project, and felt agitated and disappointed at how local politics and greed and petty squabbles were getting in the way of a real reform effort. I was complaining when my father interrupted me and said, "Could it be that you're thinking too much about what you're not getting, when you should be thinking about what you're not giving? We get what we give. Is there something that you are withholding from this enterprise?" At the close of the conversation, sensing my weariness, my dad reminded me that no act of generosity is ever wasted. He continued, "Our lives are shaped most not by what we take with us, but by what we leave behind."

Those words became a prophecy of sorts. My dad died, unexpectedly, only days later. Carlos Castaneda wrote, in one of the Don Juan allegories, "The trouble with you is, you think you have time." That is the trouble with all of us. The time is now for us to remember who we are and what we stand for, and to show up, out loud, as the givers of hope to communities in despair.

There has never been a more important time for us to enter the fray. Abuses are perpetrated in the name of the law. Too many are denied, by poverty or circumstance, access to equal justice and equal opportunity. We live in a world divided by fear. That fear can make us doubt ourselves, believing that we are somehow less than able to meet the challenges at hand. At those times, especially, we must define our mission mightily. Could it be, as Marianne Williamson so beautifully observed, that "our deepest fear is not that we are inadequate?" Could it be that "our deepest fear is that we are powerful beyond measure?"

We are here to close the gap between what is and what ought to be. We are here to be the voices of compassionate honesty in a world that is filled with too much brutality. We are here to make the difference, with use our unique expertise to give people hope. And this is what we are here for, first and foremost. To give people hope. There has never been a more important time for us to show up, in force, to work toward what we can and must achieve. At a time when so many Americans are without decent housing, health care, or a quality education, there is much to be done. Franklin Delano Roosevelt, in one of his lesser known speeches (chronicled in Cass Sunstein's *The Second Bill of Rights*) said, "Governments can err. People can make mistakes. But Dante tells us that divine justice weighs the sins of the cold-blooded and the sins of the warm-hearted on different scales. Better the occasional faults of a government, of a people, who live in a spirit of charity, than the consistent omissions of a government, of a people, frozen in the ice of their own indifference."

Let it never be said that we became frozen in the ice of indifference. What we do matters. What we say matters. Last summer, our family went up to Boston and, at Faneuil Hall, we met The Oracle, a street performer who, for a dollar, will dispense your fortune. The Oracle caught my eye, and called me over. I dutifully remitted my dollar, and he handed me a scroll. Just at this moment, the sun emerged from an otherwise gloomy sky. I opened the scroll, and on it was the message, Kind Words Conquer. I said a prayer of thanksgiving, hugged The Oracle and shouted the message out loud. Kind words do conquer. Wisdom and compassion are indivisible. Let it be said that we used our words and our actions to be instruments of healing, of kindness, and of hope.

Herbert I. London is president of the Hudson
Institute, a world-renowned think-tank in Washington, D.C. He is the former John M. Olin
Professor of Humanities at New York University. He was responsible for creating the Gal-
latin School of Individualized Study in 1972.

Herbert London is a graduate of Columbia University, 1960 and the recipient of a Ph.D. from
New York University, 1966. He is also professor
emeritus at New York University.

Chapter Twenty-Nine

The Meaning – and Demeaning – of Patriotism

Herbert I. London

In the aftermath of 9/11 patriotic sentiment was in the air. On a visit to the destruction at the World Trade Center site, some people asked if I would hold hands and sing "God Bless America." Tears rolled down my cheeks involuntarily; at that moment, I thought I knew what patriotism is.

But to some degree 9/11 has faded from our collective memory and while patriotic sentiment is occasionally evident, it has lost its immediacy. Moreover, while I once believed I was touched by the fervor of patriotism, I am now in search of its roots and meaning.

Samuel Johnson noted that "patriotism is the last refuge of a scoundrel," a quote that has filled Congressional chambers for a century or more. Alas, patriotism can be used as a cover for amoral deeds and as the justification for tyranny. Curiously the word patriotism evokes negative and positive responses.

Thomas Jefferson in a letter to his friend William Stevens Smith wrote: "The tree of liberty must be refreshed from time to time with the blood of patriots and tyrants. It is its natural manure." Alexander Pope wrote, "A patriot is a fool at ev'ry age." While William Tyler Page in *The American Creed* noted the United States… "is established upon those principles of freedom, equality, justice and humanity for which American patriots sacrificed their lives and fortunes. I therefore believe it is my duty to my country to love it, support its

"

Constitution, to obey its laws, to respect its flag and to defend it against all enemies."

From the Treaty of Westphalia, arguably the provenance of nationalism, to the present, a consensus on the meaning of patriotism has not emerged. The *American Heritage Dictionary* and *Webster's* note simply that patriotism is "love of and devotion to one's country." And patriotic is a "feeling, expressing or inspired by love for one's country."

Pegged into the historical antecedents of patriotism are words such as love, honor, loyalty, pride, devotion and sacrifice. These words clearly suggest an emotional attachment. But patriotism is also associated with reason.

In the former case, as Alexis de Tocqueville noted in *Democracy in America*, customs, traditions and a reverence for the past are emphasized; in the latter, or reasoned position, patriotism is a state of mind in which "citizens… grapple with the various aspects of America which are not so rose colored," what might be described as the oppositional side of patriotism.

The dichotomous model is found in most of the literature on the subject. Theodore Adorno, for example, distinguishes between "genuine" and "pseudo" patriot with "genuine" having a critical understanding of the nation's beliefs and "pseudo" responding with unquestioned and reflexive fealty. Others argue that there are conservative and liberal patriots. Liberal patriots believe that they must work for political change consistent with their interpretation of the national creed and conservatives maintain an uncritical allegiance to the nation and what the Founding Fathers intended.

The nation of "my country, right or wrong" intersects with nationalism or national identity since the enduring characteristics of national identity are the core values upon which the nation was founded and the attachment one feels for those values and institutions that emanated from them. Samuel Huntington in *Who Are We?* cites egalitarianism, moral traditionalism, limited government, and individualism as core principles on which the national identity rests. Obviously a patriot might use these principles as the basis for his sentiment, but patriotism is usually reserved for a specific devotion to country while national identity is a more general definition of who we are. Clearly they bleed into one another, especially when attempting to define terms.

Ernest Renan, the distinguished scholar of national identity, contends persuasively that in order to become a nation, people must indeed collectively argue to "remember" a number of things, but also to "forget" a number of things. In his sense, the fibers that weave a nation together depend on a pride in past achievements, what might be called the positive side of patriotism.

Renan relies on European examples in his analysis. However, the American case departs from its European counterparts in both national identity and patriotism. Unlike the European examples, American patriotism has a lot to do with creedal devotion, to the political ideas that inspired the founders and found expression in living documents that shaped the destiny of the nation. European nationalism and patriotism tend to be based on blood and soil, e.g. the Italian struggle for unification. The American example is predicated on faith in human possibility and a belief in a better future; by contrast, the European examples tend to be based on the glories of the past and tradition seared into human experience.

While generalizations about patriotism abound, including those to which I may be culpable, there are several dimensions that should be noted in a formal sense. If one were to extrapolate from Christopher Parker's interesting paper, "Shades of Patriotism: Group Identity, National Identity and Democracy" given at the 2003 meeting of the American Political Science Association, there are four forms of patriotism. First, there is creedal patriotism based on a belief in the doctrines that serve as a foundation for the nation. Second, there is institutional patriotism that refers to the federal system, limited government, the Congress and the law making apparatus. Third, there is reasoned patriotism (already mentioned) which refers to an analysis of achievements and flaws with the ultimate realization that positive accomplishments outdistance imperfections. Fourth, there is emotional patriotism predicated on instinct and affection rather than cost benefit calculations. What should be appreciated is that these seemingly discrete categories often overlap. Even reasoned argument and emotional attachment may coexist depending on circumstances. Immediately after 9/11 these competing belief systems often merged into a strongly held case for attachment to the American nation.

Another mitigating factor in any generalization about patriotism is that for some, group identity may inform political attitudes. If, for example, race and gender are part of the calculus, patriotism may be a function of group progress as opposed to national achievements. In other words, African Americans, to cite one case, may believe generally in the precepts of the nation, but sometimes regard the institution of slavery as a blemish on national character that affects their level of patriotism.

Clearly, perception is critical in this analysis. The patriot who fought for the Confederacy was considered a traitor when the south lost the Civil War. Clearly patriotism is associated with victory. It is also the case that belief in the nation itself is critical in the patriotic calculus. It was the notion of America that once lived in the mind of immigrants and transformed them into loyal Americans even before they landed on our shores. This was a brand image that had an ideological component and historical echoes. As John O'Sullivan notes in "The Real British Disease" (New Criterion, September 2005), the British benefited from the same condition till about 1970. Britishness served as an iconic appeal to all groups who came to serve the Crown whether Indian, Jamaican, Moslem or Christian. Needless to say, as O'Sullivan notes, a relatively recent loss of British confidence, indeed even what Britishness is, has resulted in pockets of immigrants without any attachment or allegiance to the country in which they reside. In fact, a present emphasis on multiculturalism predominates in civic Britain destroying a shared sense of national belonging.

Conditions have not evolved as dramatically in the United States, but it is also true that the U.S. is not immune from the problem of sub-group cultural isolation and challenges to patriotic fervor. Since the 1970s the dominant voice within the American Academy has worked to generate cynicism about the nature of democratic republics.

According to Keith Windschuttle in his remarkable essay "National Identity and the Corruption of History," the most dramatic manifestation of this matter occurred in 1992, the quincentenary of the discovery of the New World by Christopher Columbus. In one book after another, he notes, the European discovery was denounced as a calamity that befell native Americans and, perhaps the entire globe. In *American Holocaust: Columbus and The Conquest of the New World*, David Stannard accused Columbus of starting a process of unprecedented human destruction. Stannard wrote: "The road to Auschwitz led straight through the heart of the Americas." In *The Conquest of Paradise:*

Christopher Columbus and Columbian Legacy, Kirkpatrick Sale argues that Columbus found a land where man lived in harmony with nature and transformed it into one where he rapaciously exploited nature and exported this form of environmental abuse around the globe. This has left us, Sale notes, "at risk of imperilment – worse, the likely destruction – of the earth."

So influential is this critique that when I asked a group of my daughter's friends, who attended private schools in New York, what they could tell me about Columbus, they responded in unison that "he exported smallpox to the New World." So much for the man who brought culture, learning, science and technology to primitive civilization.

A second manifestation of the same sentiment emerged in the national history standards for American students written in 1992. George Washington made only a fleeting appearance. The founding of the National Organization for Women was considered a noteworthy event, but the first gathering of the U.S. Congress was not. What was significant for the committee that wrote these standards were the claims of oppression against women, minorities and ethnic groups rather than the achievements of the Founding Fathers. In a book written by the principals, *History on Trial*, Gary Nash, Charlotte Crabtree and Ross Dunn contend that they are intent on "a history education that is fit for a democratic society." What they mean by this is a history of discrimination, exploitation and hostility against American's sub-groups instead of a history of great men and their accomplishments.

The problem with this approach is that is an effort to falsify the past. Ending slavery or emancipating women, for instance, were morally justified and fulfilled through a reliance on the Enlightenment and Christian principles of human equality. These developments were not brought about by slaves or women, but by white Protestant men. In attempting to write history from a multicultural perspective distortions abound. The War of Independence, to cite another example, was fought and won by Protestant males, despite a feverish effort to include minorities in the struggle by historical revisionists. In fact, African Americans and Indians, to the extent they expressed an opinion on the war, almost uniformly supported the British side. Facts, however, are inconvenient when they aren't consonant with an ideological agenda adopted by historians of a revisionist bent.

Nonetheless, these revisionists have gained ground on every front and in the process have undermined the emotional side of patriotism and, alas, even the reasoned arguments for patriotism. Courses in American history and Western Civilization are increasingly bound to ideological interpretation. Even those who decry these courses are forced to be cautious for fear that extolling the values of the American nation and the civilization that gave birth to it might be seen as blind flag waving undeserving of scholarly consideration.

Another of the downsides of this historical revision is that group histories proliferate. In the United States at the moment African Americans, Mexican Americans, Japanese Americans, among others have called for histories of their own which often rely on the concept of grievance. In many of these ethnocentric programs the history of the nation is ignored. In one textbook on African-American history, Crispus Attucks, a mulatto inadvertently killed at the Boson Massacre, receives more space than Washington, Jefferson, Hamilton and Madison combined.

The spread of this "historical grievance" position is not confined to the United States and Europe. Israel is also in the throes of historical revisionism. The Jews who fled Europe seeking a refuge from the Holocaust have been recast as colonialists by scholars eager to reformulate the past on scant evidence, but with broad ideological considerations. The Six Day War has been put in the cauldron of revisionist theory and has been remodeled as a war of imperialism rather than a defensive war for survival. In each claim, there is a consequent incremental decline in the spirit that sustains patriotism. Why should anyone care about a nation of colonizers and imperialists, words that have been transmogrified into crimes?

Patriotism is refurbished by belief. In the end, even reasoned patriots who carefully weigh errors, mistakes, tragedy and achievement, must find something positive on which to hang their patriotic sentiment. The erosion of belief which afflicts the U.S. to some degree, Europe to a great degree and Israel as well, stands in stark contrast to Muslims who have a devotion to their faith and a geopolitical belief in its ultimate dominance. Perhaps this comparative examination – more than any other condition – explains why patriotism may turn out to be the overarching issue of this era.

The following timely article regarding American civics was authored by Dr. Paula A. Franzese, Professor of Law, Seton Hall School of Law, Newark, New Jersey.

<u>Chapter Thirty</u>

Bring Civics Lessons Back to the Classroom

Dr. Paula A. Franzese

We have become an uninspired people, living in a time of diminished expectations. Scandals have eroded the public trust, political corruption tests a weary electorate, and negative campaigning assaults the senses. "Gotcha" journalism, and a press hungry for the salacious and the untoward contribute to the sense that no matter how cynical you are, it's hard to keep up.

All of this malaise is as much a product of our times as it is a contributing cause. We seem to have surrendered our power, as citizens, to expect more or, perhaps most essentially, to be the inspiration that we hope to find.

Think about what we have come to view as acceptable in our homes, our workplaces, our schools, on the airwaves and in the public domain. Think about the words that we hear, the language that we use, what it is that we're watching, and who it is that we're watching.

That Paris Hilton is famous makes the point. That the protracted Anna Nicole Smith debacle has commanded the attention that it has is a wake-up call. It's time to snap out of the collective trance of complacency and self-involvement to reclaim the altruism that resides not just in some of us, but in all of us. But first it needs to be expected, and then nurtured.

Goethe made the point centuries ago: "If we treat people as they are, we make them worse. If we treat people as they could be, we help them to become what they are capable of becoming."

Part of the solution resides in a return to civics teaching in our elementary, middle and high schools. We need to be teaching our children and teenagers the essentials of character, responsibility and good government.

Ignorance, apathy, complacency

A recent Zogby International poll revealed that while a vast majority of Americans could name at least two of the seven dwarfs, fewer than 24 percent could name two U.S. Supreme Court justices. Only 42 percent could identify the three branches of government. Only one in four Americans between the ages of 18 and 34 reads a newspaper, or consults any news outlet, on a daily basis.

Ignorance, apathy and complacency are the greatest threats to democracy and to the proper and effective functioning of all three branches of government, including the fourth estate – a fair and responsible press.

Knowledge is power. Our children deserve the foundation that a good civics education can provide Honest and just leadership rests in our capacity to plan for the future by teaching our children about the promise of our participatory democracy.

We'll be able to nurture inspired future leaders and public servants to the extent that we recognize and cultivate the desire to gain power not for personal gain but for greater good. Seeds of character must be planted early on, and carefully tended.

I teach a class called Civics, Character and Leadership to sixth, seventh and eighth graders at St. Catherine's School in Cedar Grove. We talk about our system of checks and balances, the ethical responsibilities of leaders and citizens, and even how to read a newspaper. (I once asked Max Frankel, Pulitzer-prize winning journalist and former executive editor of the New York Times, "How should we read a newspaper?" He replied, "Persistently. All that the news can do is be cumulatively true." In a time of waning attention spans and instant messaging, that's important advice.)

In this civics class, we also consider the predicates to good character – being impeccable with your word, practicing principles of right speech, the power of words to hurt or to heal, and the responsible use of all avenues of communication, especially the Internet.

Recently, the New Jersey Supreme Court unanimously affirmed, in L.W. v. Toms River Regional School Boards, that students have a right to attend school without being subjected to student-on-student harassment. Significantly, the abuse chronicled in the case started in the fourth grade, when other students began referring to the then 9-year-old plaintiff as "gay," "homo" and "fag." In the fifth, sixth and seventh grades matters escalated, as other students joined in, assaulting the child with venomous words and gestures.

It's too easy to chalk up this tragedy merely to teacher or administration neglect, and certainly there was that. The fault, however, may well be in ourselves.

Our Role

There has never been a more important time for us to show up, to work toward what we can and must achieve to restore a waning polity. All of us – parents, educators, the academy, leaders, public officials, the clergy, the press, private citizens – have a role to play in the return to civics and to civility.

Civics needs to be taught, in our homes, in our schools, in courtrooms, boardrooms and caucus rooms alike.

Chapter Thirty-One

The Nature of Freedom

Hilmar von Campe

To me, the American flag is not only the flag of the United States of America, my country of choice, but also a symbol of freedom, a freedom that should be expanded to all of humanity. All human beings dream of freedom as they understand it. As somebody who once lost it along with my father, my brother and home in a totalitarian state, I appreciate a free society perhaps better than anyone who was born into it. At a breakfast of the American Retired Officer's Association in Colorado Springs I thanked the American soldiers for their battle to defeat the Nazi rule which gave me freedom.

I grew up under the Nazis, and by law, became a member of the Hitler Youth. I also fought in the German army as a gunner in a tank in the South Eastern Theater in Yugoslavia. On the other side of the front line were Soviet forces. I thought I was defending my country. As a prisoner of war in Communist Yugoslavia I escaped from my prisoner-of-war camp and crossed seven borders to unite with my family in Germany. When I crossed the demarcation line between the Soviet and the British occupation zones of Austria, I left execution or slavery behind me and stepped into freedom. It was a defining moment for my whole life even though I remained the same selfish person until I changed profoundly five years later, and found a new life and a new purpose.

I then learned that political freedom of a nation is the result of the way of life of its people. Freedom is more than the right to vote, as crucial as that right is. Freedom is a moral concept, which like God or the wind can neither be seen nor touched. We can only see and feel the consequences. Freedom is not meant for a person or a nation to go about life as they please but to be free to be truthful and to be able to give their best to others. Do we trust our government? Are we Americans free and represent a free nation? Do you love your neighbor or do you just use him? Or, like the Nazis did, do you kill him if he is in your way? For Jews and Christians alike, freedom means to be free to serve God without restriction. For America, it is her mission in the world. ...

People who lie in a democracy – and especially politicians who do so – push their nation toward a totalitarian state no matter what words of freedom and democracy they utter. All totalitarian societies are based on lies. Democracy does not lead automatically to freedom. A totalitarian society can be created by force or by vote. Hitler and the Nazis got into power by vote but without having a majority. But they knew how to manipulate other politicians and voters by lying to them. Fidel Castro came to power by military force and the help of the state department but Hugo Chavez in Venezuela has the same skill to manipulate the voters as Hitler had. In North and South America there are many politicians who lie their nations into the direction of a totalitarian system.

The point I want to make is that freedom without truth cannot last because one lie always leads to another to cover an earlier lie and so forth until total power is achieved, that means, where a society is ruled by lies and liars – a totalitarian system. A person who lies in private affairs also lies in public affairs. A president, for instance, who lies is a disaster for the battle of freedom. Why? As I said, freedom without truth cannot last. Therefore the battle for freedom is the battle for truth. Liars are enemies of freedom and since freedom is the calling and mission of this nation they are also enemies of the United States of America.

I learned this when after WWII I tried to find out how the Nazi disaster was possible in a country such as Germany where millions of people went to church on Sunday – just like me – and where millions considered themselves to be Christians, just as I did. I also wanted to know what my personal moral responsibility for this disaster was in spite of the fact that our family, beginning with my parents, detested the Nazis.

I realized that it was the lie which connected me with the Nazis. I lied to my parents, my teachers, my friends and to anybody when a lie brought me some personal advantage. The Nazis lied for political power. It was Hitler's fairy tale about the beginning of the war which made me voluntarily go to war assuming it was in defense of my fatherland against the same countries Germany fought in WWI. In reality, however, I was used by them for their godless purposes as were millions of others.

Some years ago construction started for a new house in Colorado Springs close to our backyard. Work began at six o'clock in the morning with tremendous noise. On Saturday we were awakened at the same early hour. We were looking forward to Sunday assuming that construction would not take place that day. That, however, turned out not to be the case and it became too much to me. Furiously, I went to the construction site and asked the site manager to immediately stop that noise for being Sunday. Listening to my accent the man realized that I was a foreigner. He looked at me condescendingly and said, "You know, here in America we are free!" He obviously had the wrong but popular concept of freedom, namely that it means 'I can do as I please.' His interpretation of freedom, however, didn't last long, since we knew the developer and that was the end of the early morning noise. Loving your neighbor also means to hold him to what is right.

This lie of the site manager is an example of what one might conceive as a harmless one – it affected only us and perhaps one or two more neighbors. But a lie is a lie and if this man would have looked with honesty at his life, most likely he would have found more of the same. When I did this in my life I did find a lot. But I made restitution where I could for every lie I had made or participated in. I decided that I would never lie again but stand up for truth. I also learned that every personal sin is part of creating national sins. I realized that so as I am so is my nation. No wonder that the Nazis could commit their crimes if the life of every German was similar to mine. With some friends I went through Western Europe and apologized for the harm Germany had done to their population. I was received twice by the executive director of the Holocaust Memorial Center, Rabbi Dr. David Weinstein, and apologist for the suffering we had inflicted on his people. We became friends.

People who live right will create a political and social infrastructure in their society which guarantees freedom, which is right and pleases God versus covering truth with beautiful lies to deceive society. Is, for instance, abortion right and does the law which makes it legal please God? If not, are church-goers in America like German church-goers in the thirties looking in the other direction? Don't forget the price we had to pay for it. ...

How free are we? And what do we have to do? The first step for everybody is to stop lying.

Alexander Solzhenitsyn pointed out, "The most important part of our freedom, inner freedom, is always subject to our will. If we surrender it to corruption, we do not deserve to be called human. But let us note, that the absolutely essential task is not political liberation, but the liberation of our souls from participation in the lie forced upon us, then it requires no physical, revolutionary, social, organizational measures, no meetings, strikes, trade unions. No. It requires from each individual a moral step within his or her power – no more than that. No one who voluntarily runs with hounds of falsehood will ever be able to justify himself to the living, or to posterity, or to his friends, or to his children."

Of the 56 signers of the Declaration of Independence 17 lost their fortunes, 12 had their homes destroyed, 9 fought and died, 5 were arrested as traitors, and 2 lost sons in the war. They gave everything for their freedom and for the generations to come. As Samuel Adams signed, he said, "We have this day restored the Sovereign to whom all men ought to be obedient. He reigns in heaven and from the rising to the setting of the sun, let His kingdom come." Our commitment must match theirs.

On October 11, 1798 President John Adams stated in a letter, "We have no government armed with power capable of contending with human passion unbridled by morality and religion. Avarice, ambition, revenge, or gallantry, would break the strongest cords of our Constitution as a whale goes through a net. Our Constitution was made for a moral and religious people. It is wholly inadequate for any other."

On September 21, 1924 President Calvin Coolidge in an address to the Holy Name Society stated, "It seems . . . perfectly plain that . . . the right to equality, liberty and property . . . have for their foundation reverence for God. If we imagine that swept away . . . our government could not long survive."

A future with freedom is now up to us. That we can keep it is not guaranteed. To make truth the basis of all human relationships is the task of this century. "Truth or Lies" is the ideological battle line for America and the world. There is no neutrality. You are either on the one or on the other side. Truth must be the battle cry for the second American Revolution.

America the Beautiful

Chapter Thirty-Two

History? Why?

Joy Hakim
Author of United States History Books

What's the point of studying history? Who cares what happened long ago?
After all, aren't the people in history books dead?

Those are good questions. They bother a lot of people. The bother some
people so much that they never study history. That's too bad, because those
people miss out on something very important: their own story.

History is the story of US. It tells who we are and where we have been.
Sometimes it is so surprising it jolts your mind. Here are a few answers to the
questions about studying history:

History is full of stories – true stories – the best ever. Those stories have
real heroes and real villains When you read history, you are reading about real-
life adventures.

History is a mystery. No one knows what happened in the past – at least
we don't know the whole story. We weren't there. Have you ever put a jigsaw
puzzle together? That's what learning history is like. You gather pieces of
information and try to discover how they fit. Suddenly, when you have enough
pieces in place, you begin to see the big picture. That's exciting, and so is
studying history, because new pieces of the puzzle keep fitting in.

When we read about *the mistakes people made in the past*, we can try not to make them ourselves. Nations and people who don't study history sometimes repeat mistakes.

History is especially important for Americans. In many nations – Japan or Sweden, for instance – most citizens share a common background. They have a similar look. They may worship in the same church. That isn't true of us. Some of us were once Chinese, or Italian, or Turkish, or Ethiopian. Americans don't all look alike. Sometimes we don't think alike. But as Americans we do share something. It is our history. We Americans share a common heritage. If you are an American, then the Indians, the Vikings, the Pilgrims, and the slaves are all your ancestors. You will want to know their stories.

Before we were a nation, we were ruled by England. Many Americans wanted to be free. So they wrote a Declaration of Independence explaining their goals. It begins: *We hold these truths to be self-evident, that all men are created equal, that they are endowed by their creator with certain unalienable Rights, that among these are Life, Liberty, and the pursuit of Happiness.* It also says that governments derive *their just powers from the consent of the governed.* (What does that mean?)

Consider those words about equality and happiness. In past times, governments didn't worry about things like that. Our Declaration changed ideas. It was written in 1776 and, since then, it has inspired people all over the world in battles for freedom and fairness.

Which brings me to this book's theme. It is this: *I believe the United States of America is the most remarkable nation that has ever existed. No other nation, in the history of the world, has ever provided so much freedom, so much justice, and so much opportunity to so many people.*

Some people will tell you of evil forces in the United States. They will tell of past horrors like slavery and war. They will tell of poverty and injustice today. They will be telling the truth.

The United States isn't perfect. Far from it. Being fair to everyone in a large nation is very difficult. (Do you treat everyone you know equally? How about people you don't like?) The U.S. government has made some terrible mistakes. It is still making mistakes. But usually this nation can, and does, correct its mistakes. That is because we are a democracy: power belongs to the people, not the rulers. We are also a nation governed by law, and that is very important. No one is above the law. Everyone – the president, congressmen, congresswomen, and you – lives by the same laws.

Our top – or supreme – law is the Constitution. Even bad presidents and congresses obey the Constitution. They have to. They can be impeached – which means "brought to trial" – if they don't.

The Constitution of the United States was the first national constitution written by ordinary people who intended to govern themselves. It starts with, "We the People . . ." You are part of "the People."

The Constitution's writers knew they were human and that their work might need improving. They made sure the Constitution could be changed through amendments. Right away there were 10 amendments (called the Bill of Rights) that guarantee basic freedoms. The first amendment gives you the right to worship, or not, as you wish (not as the government tells you). It protects your right to say or write what you want. You can criticize the government and not worry about being thrown in jail. That isn't true in many countries. (Check those amendments to know your other rights.)

But the Constitution didn't protect all Americans. It allowed slavery. That was a horrible mistake. We had to fight an awful civil war before the 13th amendment – ending slavery – could be passed.

Justice is fairness. Having the same laws *for all* is fair.

In the United States you are free to do anything that anyone else can do. You can run for president, be an artist, write books, or build houses.

But being a citizen of a free nation isn't easy. Free citizens are expected to be informed and think for themselves. Having rights means having responsibilities. It means asking questions and learning so that you can vote intelligently. Nations are constantly tested by those who want to upset or criticize or conquer. A good way to handle those attacks is with history's information.

The more you study history, the more you will realize that all nations are not the same. Some are better than others.

Does that seem like an unfair thing to say? Maybe, but I believe it.

I don't believe that people in one nation are better than those in another. Every nation has a mixture of good and bad people.

So why, if people are the same, are nations different?

Ideas have a lot to do with it. Nations stand on their ideas. We're lucky. The architects who designed this nation had sound ideas. They were looking for liberty, justice, and opportunity when they came here. The made sure the United States provided them.

Then they did something never done before: they created a people's government. Some men and women in other parts of the world thought that was impossible. After all, it was an unrated idea. But America's citizens proved that government by the people can work.

Chapter Thirty-Three

Land That I Love

James F. McGuire
Retired FBI Agent
Arlington, VA

America means home to me. It means freedom to live my life in accordance with a justly formed conscience. As a child, it meant freedom to roller skate back and forth to grammar school and to church. Freedom to play baseball, football, hockey, and to seek out higher education. As an adult, it meant freedom to serve my country voluntarily in time of national need, here and on foreign soil (Korea), and on safe return, freedom to marry a lovely wife and raise a large family, with deep respect for God and country and for others who occupy this planet. Many, around the world less fortunate, look to America as the land of opportunity, and have made their ways to America, overcoming many hardships, to receive citizenship in our country, a real privilege which I obtained by reason of birth under the red, white, and blue, and forever it may stand. Service to my country was my choice and protection of our freedoms has been my profession. At 17, I enlisted in the USMC, followed by a second tour in later years, as a USMC officer, which took me to Korea. This was followed by a full career as a Special Agent of the FBI.

Now almost 79 years of age, I have the same burning love and respect for God and country, for our Constitution, for our freedoms, as taught to me by my parents, early on, and reinforced through my service and experience in the USMC, FBI, and in other areas of law enforcement.

In the past few years, I have experienced major health problems, and two of my granddaughters of college age communicated with a mutual friend, a First Lieutenant, USMC, then stationed in Iraq, and told him of their grandfather's health challenges and his former USMC service.

Under the date of 13 June, 2007, from Iraqi, I received a letter forwarded to me via my granddaughters and it reads:

"Sir,

I have been meaning to send you our Battalion Battle coin, but as Taylor and Anna will tell you, I was slightly preoccupied for a good while here in Iraq. As I know you are all too well aware, war is hell and for me, it has been that and some, losing 2 Marines, and coming way too close to being a gold star son myself. I have seen what war can do and how awful it is. On the other hand, my experience has also shed light on many other things, all of them quite positive. I know that you are not feeling all too well at this point, considering what you are going through, but I wanted to take a few minutes to thank you. As a young Marine who has seen so much, I have a new and greater appreciation for "The Old Breed" Marines like you. If it hadn't been for you and your brother Devil Dogs, I would not be over here carrying such a special, pride-filled, and honor-bound tradition, and of that I mean the tradition of a Great Nation and more-so of our beloved Corps! So thank you from the bottom of my heart for doing your part when it was your time and for trusting us young Marines to carry on the proud legacy which you helped build.

I have enclosed our Battalion Coin, our Chaplain's Coin, and the coin General Conway, our Commandment, presented to me here in April, after I escorted him on his tour of our battle space. I can only hope that holding these small pieces of the corps can help you find that warrior spirit that I know still lives inside of you to help you to "stay in the fight." Feel better sir, you are in our thoughts. Semper Fidelis!"

Chapter Thirty-Four

Personal Patriotic Expressions

Written by
Various Patriotic Americans
Based on the topic
"What America Means to Me"

This chapter reflects the patriotic expressions written by various individuals, all of whom are proud of America, proud to be called Americans and proud of America's
heritage, culture and humanity.

This chapter contains the genuine, sincere, patriotic expressions of various proud, loyal Americans, whose heartfelt words reflect an exemplary love and respect for an unshakeable allegiance to the United States of America, and to the republic for which it stands, one nation under God, indivisible, with liberty and justice for all.

As you are about to read the following patriotic expressions, let us dwell for a moment on the description of patriotism by two great men, of another era, as set forth in "The New Dictionary of Thoughts," Standard Book Company, 1959.

Daniel Webster said: "Let our object be our country, our whole country, and nothing but our country. And, by the blessing of God, may that country itself become a vast and splendid monument, not of oppression and terror, but of wisdom, of peace and of Liberty, upon which the world may gaze with admiration forever."

Ralph Barton Perry said: "Those who have not risen to the level of patriotism are not likely to rise to higher levels."

What America Means To Me
I Cried With Pride
Rocco DiPippo
Freelance Political Writer

On September 11, 2007, I was in New York City attending that year's 9/11 memorial service at Ground Zero. The air was damp and raw, punctuated by torrential downpours and gusty thunderstorms. The weather reinforced the somber mood of the day.

After hours of standing outside in the wind and rain, I left the outdoor memorial services and walked to a small church, about a block way, to quiet my mind and to escape the elements.

I arrived there in time for a concert honoring the victims and heroes of September 11, 2001. As I took a seat in a second row pew facing the small choir assembled on the altar, a pianist began playing familiar notes. The choir joined him, and a proud, soaring rendition of our national anthem, the Star Spangled Banner, filled the inside of the old church to bursting.

I do not cry easily. From the opening verse until the last note of the National Anthem echoed into silence, tears ran down my face like the rain sweeping across New York City cleaning the sacred ground where the Twin Towers had once stood. I cried thinking of six years earlier, when 3,000 of my countrymen had been swept away by evil men who hated America and her freedom. I wept because their brutal act had caused so much pain, and because on that day six years past, decent ordinary people had been made to die, or made to live forever with the curse of having looked into the Devil's eyes.

And I cried because I was proud – proud that America, which had taken a terrible blow, had remained standing. Proud of my countrymen, who when faced with terror, confusion and uncertainty, had showed bravery and defiance and unity. Proud of the men and women who, even as the dust of the Towers still hung low over Manhattan, dropped their plows to take up arms to avenge the murder of their countrymen and to defend a revolutionary idea; that men should be free to pursue life, liberty and happiness without interference or coercion from their government.

Among all the nations that have passed through history, the implementation of that revolutionary idea is uniquely American, and it has made America unique among nations. That idea formed a place where practically anything is possible; where all one needs is vision and drive to accomplish what it is in life they desire to do. That revolutionary idea has been tested and proven viable by the millions of immigrants who have come to America with little more than the clothes on their backs and prospered under her freedom.

During my travels through the Middle East, I have often seen men drop their heads and lower their voices in fear while speaking to me about their leaders and their governments. And in many countries I have seen hard working men and women denied the fruits of their labors because they did not belong to the "right" family or race or tribe. Each time I witness these things, I think of America's freedom and how blessed I've been to live under it: In America men and women can criticize their leaders without fear of retribution. In America men and women are free to be themselves, free to choose their occupations, free to live where they choose to, free to practice the religion of their choice or to practice none at all, free to love who they want to, free to do just about anything, as long as it does not infringe on another person's right to do the same.

That is the meaning of America and that is its promise: not that "all men are created equal," – because clearly all men are created unequal – but that in spite of that natural, inherent inequality, all men shall be treated equally under the law and afforded the same set of rights so that they might freely express their God-given individual natures.

As I listened to the choir on that rainy September day, those thoughts entered my mind and calmed my soul.

When the last notes had been sung, I left the small church and headed back towards Ground Zero. As I walked I saw thousands of people wandering the wet New York City streets. They were people from all walks of life, free to pursue their lives as they saw fit.

That kind of freedom is worth any price.

What America Means To Me

Kevin Null
(Grandson of the author)
Ramsey, New Jersey

When I was much younger, I had heard that my grandfather and his brothers served in World War II, but they never talked about what they had done. My grandfather first served in North Africa with the Air Force, then his unit joined the 15th Air Force in Southern Italy. My Uncle Roy went to some small islands near Russia and my Uncle Henry was stationed in England and was in the second wave of infantry troops to land in Normandy, France.

A few years ago, I traveled with my parents and sister to Normandy, France. As I stood near the cliffs I could see the English Channel and I began to think about what took place on the beach below on June 6, 1944. That was called D-Day, or Departure Day from England to invade and destroy the German troops that were heavily armed and hiding in bunkers on the French Coast of Normandy. Fortunately, my uncle managed to survive and eventually returned home as did my other uncle and grandfather after the war ended in May 1945.

After looking at the English Channel and the once-bloody beaches, I turned and walked to the Normandy American Cemetery. It is approximately 172 acres and contains the bodies of over nine thousand men and women. There are three Medal of Honor winners buried there.

The area of the cemetery is rectangular with the main paths laid out in the pattern of a Latin Cross. As we entered the cemetery we first went to the visitors building, where veterans could sign the Veteran's Book, and other people like us could sign the main Visitor's Book.

Then we walked to the Memorial, which is a 22-foot bronze statue of an American youth rising from the waves. On each side of the statue are huge wall maps showing the various battles that took place in Europe during the war.

Behind the statue is the Garden of the Missing, which pays tribute to over a thousand soldiers, sailors and airmen who fell in Normandy and have no known grave.

From this point, we entered the main area of the cemetery and followed the path to the Chapel. This is built from limestone and the main inscription reads: "I Give Unto Them Eternal Life and They Shall Never Perish."

The cemetery borders on the left flank of Omaha Beach and overlooks the area where the First Division landed on D-Day.

As we looked at the cemetery we were overcome with emotion thinking of all the young men and women who gave their lives for our freedom. Every cross was identified and in perfect even rows. Most of the dead were from the actual landings on June 6, 1944, while others were from nearby beach battles.

It was in a sense a sad yet proud experience for me because it helped to make me realize how precious freedom is and how grateful we should always be to the men and women who died so that we might live. I will never lose sight of the meaning of the field of the white crosses.

What America Means To Me

Philip A. McNiff
Executive Vice President, New York Yankees
Tampa, Florida

How could an individual be more fortunate than myself and my family?

I was born in the United States of America to patriotic and God-fearing parents. They taught me through words and example to praise God and love our country. There was always great respect for the American flag and our country's traditions.

In America, one can set personal goals and pursue them through devotion and hard work. Goals can be achieved, as evidenced by our country's forefathers.

Thank God for my parents' love of America and guidance they furnished regarding patriotism and religion. I hope to pass these values onto my children.

What America Means To Me

George M. Steinbrenner III
Owner, New York Yankees
Tampa, Florida

To me, America means "human freedom." Where men have the opportunity to venture for themselves and be assured of all the gains and take all the losses. A country where men are able to think, speak and worship freely. America is a country where men can maintain a difference of opinion with government and still continue to live under the protection of habeas corpus.

What America Means To Me

Lou Ferrarese
Business Executive
Demarest, New Jersey

Maybe it is because I am from immigrant parents, both parents born in Bari, Italy, that my feelings for America are one of thanks. Thank God my parents had the courage to come to America and allow me to enjoy the riches of this wonderful country.

When I think of America I look at what this country has endured to become the nation that it is and I am thankful. The brave men and women, who fought and sacrificed because they loved their country so, I thank them.

When I think of America I look at its people, their diversity and loyalties and I am thankful.

When I think of America I look at its form of government and say thank God I live in this great nation.

When I see a soldier or I hear our national anthem or see our flag flying high or say the pledge of allegiance I count my blessings and feel grateful and yes, thankful.

The fact that God shed His grace on America, I am thankful.

One can equate America with the Garden of Eden in that we are free to choose our own destiny as long as we obey the laws of the land. We are a truly free society and am therefore thankful to the Lord.

What America Means To Me

Peter Russo
Editor – Ediblog.com

America's greatness (and magnanimity) is the direct result of its Judeo-Christian heritage. It has been the motivating force behind its willingness to sacrifice life and limb in order to bring the light of democracy to the darkest corners of the globe.

And as a result: America is the greatest experiment the world has ever witnessed.

What America Means To Me

Saurabh Patel
An Indian Immigrant's Perspective
Rockaway, New Jersey

America, in essence, is "the land of the free and the home of the brave." This phrase is a phrase we Americans have always strived to accomplish. It is because of this, that people look to our country with hope from all around the world. If we weren't able to keep our promises, our country would've fallen right after it had been formed. We, as citizens, strive to uphold the legacy that our founding fathers created. That is why, when we travel to another country, we can proudly declare that we are Americans without being scorned. Except for our own Civil War, we Americans never changed the beliefs that were written in the Declaration of Independence. Looking at other great countries you could see a significant amount of change occurring through various times in history, often creating conflict or a change in power. Ours has been a tradition since the beginning, and it shall remain so for ages to come.

From the perspective of a non-native of America, he/she could say that many aspects of American life are very different than what he/she had been used to. One might say that the quality of life and healthcare are very strong in America. Because of a better life, it brings many different careers and opportunities that might not have been possible previously. It is because of these many opportunities that helped us become a world superpower since World War II. The foundation of America was no different then, and I don't see any reason why it should ever change.

Another very important factor that contributes to the success of America is education. Here in this land, education brings students freedom unlike any others, and gives them a comfortable environment where they can really do anything without the constant worry of time constraints. Unparalleled education ties in with the vast number of career opportunities that are available to students.

Many countries ask why Americans are so rich and successful. Our proud answer is that we took chances to make a better life and that in turn led to our greatness.

What America Means To Me:
America – We Hear Your Cry

Dieter Pfisterer
CEO, Pfister Maintenance & Energy, Inc.
Paterson, New Jersey

Where has justice and liberty for all gone?

How did it happen that schools have to teach in different languages, ignoring English, and stores throughout the country display signs in foreign languages? How is it that instructions on a great deal of merchandise are printed in many languages – increasing the cost to us all – oh, America, I hear you crying.

How can it be that politicians ignore their constituents and redistribute our hard earned income and leave our borders unprotected? How does Congress continue to denigrate our sitting president and call members of our military murderers and betrayers? – Oh, America, I hear you crying.

When our legal system and our judges make laws instead of interpreting our Constitution, when judges allow pedophiles to roam free with just a slap on their wrist for their crimes against children, when midnight pork barrel spending is out of control and becomes the order of the day in Congress, when the approval rating of our legislative body is the lowest in history and when our election process costs billions of dollars and takes years to complete – oh, America, I hear you crying.

How can the few lead the majority astray?

What is America to me? It is the home of freedom, a home free of oppression, the ability to exercise freedom of choice – religion, beliefs, opinions, speech, political affiliation and more. It means the government's responsibility is to keep its citizens and its borders safe and to enforce all laws already on the books regarding illegal immigration, and those laws initiated to protect against terrorism. America is one nation, under God, with one official language. It has a legal system which should always be constrained in seeking enormous punitive settlements and uncompromising in turning away from frivolous lawsuits. America should have judges who enforce the laws and not manufacture laws to suit their personal agendas.

To be an American is to vote for politicians who work for and on behalf of the people without regard to attaining power or political self interest. America is a place where the educational system was always second to none. America's medical system is still the best in the world, and should be allowed to remain so, free from continual fear of lawsuits. America is a country where there is room for respectful disagreement over any and all issues, the key being with respect and tolerance.

America is capitalism at its best, and the ability for anyone to make it to the top through hard work and determination. It is where a famous president once stated, "Ask not what your country can do for you, but what you can do for your country," and where our political parties can work harmoniously for the good of the country.

This is what America means to me. Before it is too late, let us wipe away America's tears and work to retain liberty and justice for all along with the inalienable right for our voice to be heard to keep intact all of the reasons why America is the greatest democracy on the face on the earth.

What America Means To Me

Paul J. Batura
Senior Assistant to the Chairman, Focus on the Family
Colorado Springs, Colorado

A simple yet profound question is the one upon which this noble editorial undertaking is based. For how does a proud and humbled citizen of these United States encapsulate in just a few short words the meaning and magnificence of America?

My beloved country remains the fulfilled promise of its founders and a gift of God from whom all good things come. A productive American life is best punctuated by a commitment to honest work, a devotion to responsibility of various stripes and a tireless and tenacious willingness to sacrifice self for the sake of the Union. America needs much more, but she deserves no less. She is neither fragile nor feeble, but requires our regular care and continued self control. If we can manage to manage ourselves, our country will reap the benefits of a measured and tempered life. Self-government has never worked without self-discipline.

And so, America means more to me than words can capture, but she is, indeed, the last great hope of this world – and yet still *our* hope for years to come. May we remain worthy of her representation. May all who find security within her borders be granted the protection of life, the privilege of her liberty and remain ever in pursuit of the happiness that only the Creator of the world can grant.

What America Means To Me

John P. DiMarchi
LT. US Navy, 1942-1946
Special Agent FBI, 1947-1978 (Ret)
New Milford, New Jersey

To ask this question of a son whose parents immigrated to America during 1913 and whose marriage resulted in 5 children, 11 grandchildren, 12 great-grandchildren and 4 great-great-grandchildren, is like asking, would I like to be healthy? Would I like to be wealthy? – or do I like vanilla ice cream?

America to me means attending a Yankee baseball game and watching the kids eating hot dogs and listening to the tremendous outbursts of enthusiasm as the Yankees score and then listening to "God Bless America" as chills run up and down my spine.

Getting up Easter morning and watching the ladies leave church in their stylish hats.

Watching the Army slogan, "Be All You Can Be" on TV and realizing where else can such a saying be so possible, but in America.

Entering a small town such as Hibbing, Minnesota, or Tifton, Georgia, in the wee hours of the morning, and watching the shops open, the store windows being washed – not to forget the loud and sincere "good morning" as you enter the local café for breakfast.

The realization that millions of persons throughout the world are dying for the opportunity to come to the shores of America just to enjoy the local café for breakfast.

The realization that millions of persons throughout the world are dying for the opportunity to come to the shores of America just to enjoy these freedoms that we take for granted.

The glorious sunset that I see each night as I watch the Rocky Mountain foothills from my residence in Boulder, Colorado.

The grateful feeling that I experience each morning as I rise and watch a breathtaking view of the sun gloriously rise, as I thank God for one more day.

The realization that all of this was made possible because of a firm belief in the existence of God and that my parents immigrated to America.

God bless America.

What America Means To Me

William E. Sprague, M.D.
Grand Rapids, Michigan

In my country, America, I am constantly reminded of my freedom to speak of what I have to say. To listen to those who feel and speak differently than I and be accepting of what they have to say although I may not agree. I have defended my country and its beliefs as a young soldier in World War II. Our Lady Liberty sends a beacon for all the world to be witness to America. Although with certainty we are far from perfection we stand tall. When I disagree with our elected officials I will speak of my beliefs as an American. As a volunteer physician who has traveled extensively to the poorest countries in the world, it reconfirms my love for America as a great global benefactor. As my journey of life continues I will continue to speak for a peaceful world rather than be witness to the terror that threatens us.

What America Means To Me

Ed Petersen
Retired FBI Agent, Former Director of Security for Major League Baseball,
Managing Partner with Buckley-Petersen Global
Allendale, New Jersey

America means so much to me. I often reflect upon how blessed I am having the opportunity to live in our great country. When I pick up the newspaper and read about all of the problems throughout the world, I realize that America is a very special place. I know we as a country have our share of faults, differences and at times express strong opinions on matters that are important to us. However, through it all, I see the value of our democratic system, our way of life and how American people are so quick to respond when others are in need anywhere in the world.

I like to think back on what it must have been like for our ancestors to come into New York Harbor and see for the first time the Statue of Liberty. The feeling inside of them to know they had arrived in the land of opportunity, the land of the free. The inscription on the statue proclaims, "Give me your tired, your poor, your huddled masses yearning to be free." What a message to this great melting pot of different nationalities, races and religions. I think that is what makes America so special, the diversity, people coming from all over the world to make a better life for themselves and their families.

As Americans we must always remember the sacrifices of others in helping to preserve our freedoms, rights, values and personal safety. I thank God every day for all of his blessings. Being an American is certainly a blessing we shouldn't take for granted.

What America Means To Me

Jim Johnson
Producer – Phoenix Communications
Whitehouse, New Jersey

America means all the little things in life that are good. It means a summertime of fun – going to Little League games or playing softball, or simply sitting on the deck with a cold beer in the summer, knowing that the lawn awaits but that the grass will be there to be cut tomorrow.

Soon, the days get shorter and cooler, but it's time for football, and pumpkins, and the great color of the leaves in the fall, and the sound they make after they fall to the ground when you take that brisk walk in the autumn air. It's that feel and smell – that's America.

Before you know, it's time for Christmas carols and colors. It's burning logs in the fireplace. The magic of that first snowfall of the year, and the sledding and hot chocolate that follows.

That's more America.

And is there anything quite like the first crocus in the spring? When life starts all over again. When that ugly crabapple tree in the yard turns a brilliant pink – if only until the first rainfall that follows. And cabin fever is over and kids are out riding bikes.

It all sounds so corny, but these are things we can do in America. And although many complain about what is wrong here, the positives far outweigh the negatives. What's better than *our* simple pleasures? And tell me a place where folks can enjoy such simplicity more than in America? No such place exists, and I thank God that many have sacrificed so much for our good fortunes.

What America Means To Me

Dr. Sung Bae Ju
Opera Singer
Wayne, New Jersey

I am proud to call America, my new homeland where both of my daughters, Hannah and Sarah, were born. I came to America to study music and eventually became an opera singer. My family members are determined to be good American citizens and to gradually assimilate everything that is American.

I am convinced that America desires to protect the rights and freedom for everyone while at the same time provide equal opportunities for everyone. America respects honest, law-abiding people in accordance with the Constitution of the United States.

We are indebted to all the brave American soldiers who fought and those who sacrificed their lives in World War II, Korea, Vietnam, Afghanistan and Iraq. I am aware of America's aid and assistance given to South Korea, a country that now enjoys a massive economic growth. I am also aware that it is the desire of America that there should be a peaceful reunification between South and North Korea.

Since I arrived in America, I have learned that this is truly a beautiful country that affords anyone and everyone an opportunity to succeed. I have had the honor to be associated with some dedicated hard working politicians, such as the Honorable Scott Garrett and members of his staff as well as someone, whom I refer to as my American sister, Charlotte Vandervalk, a very capable Assembly Lady in the State of New Jersey.

My family and I have been honored to have served our community at various times with our musical talents. We have been given the opportunity to sing at such places as the Veterans Home, the FBI Headquarters in Newark, New Jersey, the U.S. Attorney's Office in New Jersey, the Asian Pacific Islander Heritage Celebration and many other social affairs. We are grateful for the expression of interest and respect shown by Americans toward the cultures of other countries. We are most grateful to the members of the FBI, and police officers, who protect us night and day.   We are especially grateful to Mr. Weysan Dun,

Special Agent In Charge of the Newark, New Jersey, FBI Office, who spoke at a gathering held at the Korean American Churches Council of New Jersey, where he was warmly received.

We are aware that people engaged in the field of law enforcement continue to make America safe and secure, my family and I hope that by lending our musical talents at various social events, we are also contributing to the well-being of America the Beautiful. As we look to the future we hope that in a small way we will be able to add to the beauty of America and what it stands for with our voices so that everyone might be able to dream beautiful dreams with the hope they can attain their goals.

Yes, I am proud to be an American and proud to say this is what America means to me.

What America Means To Me

Bob DiBiasio

Vice President of Public Relations/Cleveland Indians

My grandparents on my father's side came to America from an area of Italy between Naples and Rome called Casserta as non-English speaking immigrants with no formal education.

Nothing was more important to my father than his Italian heritage. It was through that heritage he and my mother (the daughter of Italian immigrants, as well) taught my two brothers and me to embrace important traditions such as:

- A strong faith in people
- A strong pride in family achievements
- And, of course, a passion for food

Blessed to have parents who were partners in life – my mother and father were married for 57 years until my father's passing in 2002. They provided my brothers and me with three valuable but simple lessons:

- How to care … to treat others as we wish to be treated- with respect and dignity.
- How to share … to serve God and our community in all that we do.
- To be fair … it is important to remember to leave enough for others.

It is the most precious gift of our Italian heritage.

And it is a wonderful legacy that began with two immigrants with no formal education, but a passion for life and the spirit to provide their children and grandchildren with the opportunity to grow to their full potential.

The key word above is opportunity – that is *What America Means To Me*.

The Land of Opportunity—via education:

Education was a value hard-wired into our family by our grandparents who understood that opportunity was best experienced through America's free public education system.

Grandma and Grandpa "D" had four sons—three of whom went on to college and earned post-graduate degrees. The one son who did not go on to college (my uncle Jimmy) was the second oldest and had to go to work to help pay for the eldest son's college education at Oberlin College, as well as save for the college education of the two younger brothers.

Each of the four DiBiasio sons had three children—10 of the 12 children have earned advanced degrees. There is a lawyer, three PhD's, five Master's Degrees and a Masters of Divinity. Included in that group is my oldest brother, Dr. Daniel A. DiBiasio, who is President of Wilmington College in Wilmington, Ohio, and the middle brother, Dr. Anthony J. DiBiasio III, a child psychologist in Cleveland, Ohio.

Public education made our father's success, as he dedicated more than 50 years of his life to the students of Lakewood, Ohio. A life based on the belief that each and every student was special. That America's public school system was a place where creativity and imagination was encouraged and flourished.

The Land of Education—via opportunity:

My 30 years of experience in the world of Major League Baseball, 29 as the PR man for my beloved Cleveland Indians, has provided an education about American life through the diversity, shared values and shared passions for a uniquely American sport.

I have had the opportunity to travel the world, meet Presidents, leaders of business, celebrities—as well as players from all over the world and across generations. Through America's Pastime I have met fans of every ethnic group and economic class. We have helped people, changed lives and revived communities. We provide young people with the educational and recreational resources to reach their full potential and gain self-confidence.

All based on the three core values bestowed upon me by parents—to care, to share, and to be fair.

What America Means To Me

David Hughes
Executive VP-AAA North Jersey
Wayne, New Jersey

America means to me the ability of immigrants to come to this country, raise a family, work hard and allow for their children and grandchildren to become successful. My maternal grandfather, Dominick Sacco, was born in Italy in 1899. He came to this country as an infant. After returning to Italy for several years he came back to America for good sometime around 1920. He had no particular skill but because Paterson, New Jersey, was a silk dying and manufacturing center, he went into that industry as a laborer. He married my grandmother, Mary, in 1927 and my mother, Catherine, was born in 1930. He worked his way up in the business eventually becoming a master dyer by the end of his career. He probably never made more than $200 a week (which was considered good money in the '50s) but by the late '50s he owned his own home and provided a good life for his family. He allowed my mother the opportunity to grow up in a comfortable, if not wealthy, lifestyle and eventually she married my father. My parents had the ability to live better and become successful, as I have done one generation later. But that all doesn't happen without Dominick's hard work, saving for the future, moral firmness and belief in himself and his adopted country. And it also doesn't happen without the opportunities that this country provided for an unskilled young man during the early part of the last century. Dominick's story has been repeated millions of times before and since by people with names like Patrick and Juan and Kim and Solomon. Collectively they and their offspring contribute to making this country what it is... The greatest nation ever placed on this Earth.

What America Means To Me

Al Genkinger
Retired FBI Agent
Matawan, New Jersey

I was born in 1935 to Rosel Nee Hofler and Christian Genkinger, who had immigrated from Germany in the 1920s seeking a better life for themselves from the ruination existing in Germany after WWI. My father had studied to be an accountant/bookkeeper. His journey to the United States took a detour and instead he traveled first to San Paolo, Brazil, where he remained for approximately one year before continuing on to the U.S.

My parents met as a result of an introduction by a relative in the early 1930s and they both agreed not to marry until they had saved at least $1,000, which was a large amount of money in those days. It was 1933 when they married in New York City, and my sister Hannelore was born in 1934 and approximately one year later I was born. My father decided to change professions and he chose to become a butcher.

At the onset of WWII my sister and I though still very young, knew that something bad was happening. My father as a patriotic American citizen wanted to join the Merchant Marines, however my mother had to beg him not to because it was the deadly "Murmansk" run for which he had applied. The wartime years were stressful in many ways, especially if you happen to be of German extraction. While we attended school in the Bronx, we were subjected to verbal abuse by classmates as well as neighbors. This was true also of my childhood friend, Werner Wilhelm Friedricks, who always had to face a barrage of verbal abuse.

In spite of this period of discrimination, I graduated from high school and managed to attend Fordham University for a brief period before joining the Army, the 2nd Infantry Division, MP Company in Alaska from 1955 to 1957. I returned home and completed my education including a law degree from Fordham University. It was in the year 1963 that I was extended an invitation to join the FBI which I accepted and devoted 23 proud years culminating in 1986. To me, the FBI was the zenith of my achievements and loved every day I was fortunate to serve.

To this very day, my good friend Werner and I thank our lucky stars (read: God) for our lives. Werner was a twin, however his mother and twin brother died at childbirth. About the time that WWII started, Werner managed to leave Germany for the USA, just before the travel barriers were adopted. Werner became a successful Construction Engineer for IBM, and contributed to the well-being of our American society.

We still recall with astonishment all that happened during the early years of our lives and how fortunate we were to grow up in the USA. We both had heard horror stories of the deprivation that our relatives in Germany had to endure. The bombings, the lack of food, etc. and we often times think of the frightening possibility that if we had grown up there, we might not have made it through the conflict. Some people living in the USA do not realize how lucky they are to live in this great and beautiful country. I thank God that I am an American.

What America Means To Me

Jules Bonavolonta
Retired FBI Agent
Vero Beach, Florida

I've traveled a great deal over the past forty-five years. These travels have taken me to more than forty countries and I can say, without a doubt, that on each and every trip, I've come to know and understand what America means to me. I realize how blessed I've been to have been born in this country. Day after day, month after month, and year after year, for as long as I can remember, I've seen how so many people have been fighting to leave their countries and get into our country. It's caused me to say to myself so many times how lucky I am to be in a country where people are fighting, and in many cases dying, to get into. I've seen the greatness and affluence of this nation and how it uses those attributes to help so many nations and so many people suffering around the world. There is no nation that comes to the assistance of those in need as does ours. We lend our incredible support to all those who ask for it and so many more who never ask but are so happy to receive our help. And we ask for nothing in return. That's the kind of country we are.

And I speak here only of humanitarian aid. On a much more personal side, how many of our young men and women have given their lives in the cause of freedom? One could easily say too many. But that's not how we are. We do what we believe is the right thing to do and we do it whatever the cost. And, God knows, over the decades, the cost has been enormous. And still, we never complain. That's the kind of country we are.

All I have to do each and every waking morning is to consider, just for a very brief moment, what this world would look like if there were no America to understand fully and completely what America means to me and should mean to every American.

What America Means to Me

Robert J. Lenehan
Retired FBI Agent, Westfield, New Jersey

During the particularly spirited, and certainly unique, 2008 presidential primary campaign season, I am struck not only by the passion of all of the participants, candidates as well as voters, but also by our confidence in our American system of government. No matter how much we agree, or disagree, with each other, on the candidates or the issues, we proceed with confidence in this special, four-year transition of administrations, without fear of disruption or catastrophe. Our American system of government is truly a beacon and example for people everywhere who cherish freedom and the quest to live their lives in justice and equality.

I feel privileged to have served our country as a military officer and Special Agent with the FBI. For as far back as I can remember, that is what I wanted to do with my life. I feel particularly grateful to have raised our children in this special country where they are guaranteed their own choices, whatever they may be, and that they will pass this responsibility and opportunity along to their own children as well.

With these privileges and gifts come responsibility and the sure sense that none of what America is, or who Americans are, is assured without our individual contributions and sacrifices. As Americans, we have confidence in each other, and in our system of government, and know we will always try to do the right thing.

My Journey From Poverty:
What America Means To Me

Hank Garrett
Award-winning Actor, Black Belt Martial Artist

I grew up in poverty on the streets of Harlem, New York. My parents used a pushcart as peddlers of fruits and vegetables, and regularly appeared in the public market to earn a few dollars to buy food for the family.

I enjoyed listening to the radio as a child, and I was fascinated by the quick wit of comedians. I began to tell jokes to various groups of people on street corners, this of course saved me from gang beatings. In order to protect myself and fight back if I had to, I decided at the age of 13 to learn the art of weight-lifting, as a result I was able to defend myself whenever necessary. My dream to be involved in power-lifting and body-building was finally realized and soon thereafter I won the New York State Power Lifting Championship. Shortly thereafter I decided to utilize my new found strength, by engaging in the sport of wrestling and was known as the Minnesota Farmboy in spite of the fact that I had never been outside of the borders of New York state.

After five years of professional wrestling and slamming onto canvasses, I realized that comedy was much easier to do and less strain on my body. So I packed my trunks and shoes and made my way to the New York Catskill Mountains where I landed my first job as a Social Director for the then-famous Browns Hotel. Comedy is an art, that I learned to some extent, while growing up in Harlem as a boy. I enjoyed making people laugh as a result of my funny stories let alone my imitations of various characters and dialects.

As luck would have it, I was fortunate to be noticed as a comedian and began to work for such famous people as Jerry Vale, Della Reese, Frankie Lane, Tony Bennett and many others. It was fun doing shows at the Copacabana in New York City and the Sands and Stardust Hotels in Las Vegas. Then suddenly another dream came true during one of my performances. A gentleman by the name of Nat Hiken watched me perform and later asked me to audition for the part of Officer Nicholson on the famous show called, "Car 54 Where Are You."

Following this episode, I landed a part in a movie which became my signature role. The infamous Killer Postman in "Three Days of the Condor" which enabled me to win the New York Film Critics Award. Since then, I have worked with such individuals as Peter Falk, Patrick Stewart, Kathleen Turner, Christopher Lloyd, Al Pacino, Sophia Loren, James Coburn and James Earl Jones.

During all those years I had studied Karate and was inducted into the World Karate Hall of Fame, Gold Coast Hall of Fame and London Hall of Fame and Black Belt in several systems. I was attached to the Marine Corps as an entertainer, and traveled overseas many times to help add a little laughter to our fighting Marines.

Yes, I grew up in poverty in the streets of Harlem, where I had witnessed much suffering for want of food and jobs, but I was determined to find my way, however possible. Telling jokes was my stepping stone to greater things, entertainment, wrestling, weight and power lifting, yet what gave me the greatest personal satisfaction was being able to bring a smile on the many faces of our beloved Marines. Only in America can one achieve much sought after goals. This is America, this is the land I love, and for sure, this is what America means to me.

What America Means To Me

Sharon Hughes
Radio Host & President, "The Center For Changing Worldviews"

America is the land, not just of my home, but of my heart. Why? Because I understand the hard-won freedoms that make America so unique and great. Both sets of my grandparents came to the United States on boats from Eastern European countries to escape oppressive governments. My father fought in WWII to protect the highly valued liberty we enjoy. My husband served both in Vietnam and in three runs for public office. And together we work to keep the true American dream alive in the public square. Why? Because we understand for America to continue to remain unique and great for future generations, it takes the investment of American citizens, like those who have gone before us, like you and like me.

What America Means To Me

Robert F. McDonnell
Governor of the State of Virginia

America means principles – fundamental principles planted at Jamestown, tempered by our Revolutionary Way, and refined in the furnace of our struggles for equality.

America means the dignity and worth of the individual – a simple belief, yet mighty enough to defeat the tyranny of foreign powers, break the chains of discrimination in our own land, and provide the unalienable basis for the liberties enjoyed by all.

America means a Republic – a limited government guided by the precepts of the Declaration of Independence, framed by the parameters of our Constitution, and regulated by our Bill of Rights.

America means free and open markets – the entrepreneurial liberty that turned a wilderness into the greatest free enterprise system the world has ever known.

America means faith – the belief that our rights and liberties come not from an enlightened state but from the hand of God.

America means a scarlet thread of freedom coursing through our history. America has been freedom's defender against tyrannies of all shades. America has been freedom's advocate against false philosophies. America has been freedom's guardian against assaults from all corners of earth. America has been freedom's home in times of tumult.

Above all, America means promise – a promise secured by the blood of patriots spilt on battlefields around the globe, a promise fulfilled, expanded, and manifested by the faith and actions of our Fathers, and a promise of ever more freedom, prosperity, and opportunity for future generations.

My America
The Past, The Present and The Future:
What America Means To Me

Bill D'Urso
Special Agent (Retired Bureau of Diplomatic Security)

U.S. Department of State

Being born during the Great Depression in 1934 and growing up in Hamden, Connecticut (a suburb of New Haven), I grew up during the second World War. At the age of seven, I vividly remember the radio announcement informing the people of the U.S. that the Japanese had bombed Pearl Harbor. On that fateful day, even at my tender young age, I was gripped by the spirit of the adults around me. As usual, we were at my immigrant grandparents' house on that Sunday, December 7, 1941.

I come from a large Italian family, with a lot of uncles, most of whom have since passed on, but two who are still with us, are both WWII veterans. One served in the U.S. Marine Corps and made landings on Saipan, Tinian, Kwajalean and Iwo Jima. The other served in the U.S. Navy aboard the carrier Yorktown.

All of my friends had relatives fighting in the war. President Roosevelt was our leader and we saluted the flag every morning and said a prayer before classes started. Lest anyone think this was in a parochial school, it was in the public schools. Of course, anyone who did not want to say a prayer was free to do so. Imagine, we saluted the flag, sang God Bless America, America the Beautiful or the National Anthem and we weren't damaged. How unique.

In my circles, we were products of hard-working, average, middle class parents. We had little money but a lot of family. My folks bought their first car when I was nineteen and on my way to the Marine Corps. Walking was a means of travel for school, church and recreation. We played football and baseball in empty lots and hockey on frozen ponds. No little leagues and no one came to see us play. No umpires or referees. Who cared? We played for fun and had a great time. Our heroes were our parents, the guys fighting the war and serving the country. Unlike today, the movie people also served. Stars such as Jimmy Stewart, Clark Gable,

Lee Marvin, Glen Ford and on and on served and put it all on the line. The same was true of the sports stars, Ted Williams, Joe DiMaggio, Phil Rizzuto, Art Donovan, Chuck Bednarick, all served their country. This is why we could identify with them. They were the same as us, as we took our turn in serving the country.

I look at my twelve grandchildren today and wonder who they can identify with in Hollywood or the sports world. Not many come to mind, except for Pat Tillman, who gave up a multi-million dollar contract to play professional football, to join the Army and serve the country. I also see my grandchildren looking at a country with diminished freedom. I'm not talking about things like the Patriot Act. That is a necessity of war. I'm talking about the continued effort of those that want to take over every facet of our life. What kind of car we can drive, one source for healthcare, continuous raising of taxes and on and on. Looking to the government to solve every problem is not conducive to the freedom we have known in this country.

In spite of this, I know we are the greatest country in the world. How do I know this? One reason is the fact that everyone wants to come here. You rarely hear of anyone wanting to leave and those that threaten to leave, never do. Another reason is, in my career, I have traveled to over 100 countries, in every area of the world. I have never found any I would rather live in, or be from.

America has risen to the occasion so many times to preserve freedom around the world, whether it was fighting fascism in WWII or communism in the Cold War. We have risen to the occasion to aid foreign nations in distress, whether it be a natural disaster or a man-made disaster. Uncle Sam is always there. No matter what the critics say. Most of them are America haters. The most poignant example today is those that berate us for fighting the terrorists of the world. They are the same ones who helped turn the people against the Vietnam War. In spite of the fact that we never lost on the battle field, we lost that war because the will to win was lost through the media and politics.

I still believe as President Ronald Reagan believed, that we are a shining beacon and those that would like to see a world of dictators know this and why we have been under constant attack from them throughout our history. It is why I still get a thrill and a feeling of pride when I see a parade of our fine warriors of today marching or attend a ball game and hear the National Anthem. As our 26th president, Theodore Roosevelt said:

It is not the critic who counts: not the man who points out how the strong man stumbles or where the doer of deeds could have done better. The credit belongs to the man who is actually in the arena, whose face is marred by dust and sweat and blood, who strives valiantly, who errs and comes up short again and again, because there is no effort without error or shortcoming, but who knows the great enthusiasms, the great devotions, who spends himself for a worthy cause; who, at the best, knows, in the end, the triumph of high achievement, and who, at the worst, if he fails, at least he fails while daring greatly, so that his place shall never be with those cold and timid souls who knew neither victory nor defeat.

In today's world, that probably sounds corny to some, but to me, it describes our country and why we are, and hopefully, will always be the greatest and most free country in the world. This is what America means to me.

What America Means To Me

Gil Alba
Retired First Grade Detective NYPD, Owner of Alba Investigations,

FBI/NYPD Task Force...Made numerous appearances on National TV/Radio

Somers, New York

Puerto Rican-born and at the age of four, I arrived in New York City with my mother and brother in 1948. Truly a proud American, I am.

During the tumultuous years the rights of "life, liberty, and the pursuit of happiness" as is stated in the Declaration of Independence, was indeed challenged. If, as Thomas Jefferson said, a little revolution is healthy now and again, then the late '60s and early '70s were robust times indeed.

I had to become "blue" before I first experienced the bias, anger and frustration in our own country, but truly a proud American, I am.

In 1968, a year which lay at the center of an era of various social and political revolutions, I became a New York cop. The Vietnam War with our young soldiers returning in body bags and the civil rights movement were lighting up our TV screens with violence, assassinations, cities burning.

In addition, the age of Aquarius was upon us—all authority—civil, moral, religious—was to be thrashed. There were to be no more rules, no more repression—freedom (The notion that true freedom requires personal responsibility was lost.). Lastly, the women's movement and the fledgling gay rights movement were gaining steam. What a time to wear a badge! What a great time to personify law and order!

Cops became "pigs," and were characterized as everything except what I believed them and knew them to be—protectors of all citizens, people who were literally willing to die for strangers. I thought my chosen profession to be honorable, noble, and yes, heroic, but few other than police officers, were of like mind, yet truly a proud American I am.

The evolution of America brought change, the world changed, I'm different, but never, ever indecisive about my America.

Our nation's defenses have been compromised by the evil forces of terrorism. My beloved city was attacked on 9/11. Crushed us? No, merely proceeded to make our country more patriotic, more united with a deeper understanding that we are a great nation.… Religious freedom gives us a right to pray… God bless America.

What America Means to Me

John D. Glover,
Retired FBI Agent

America, our dichotomous country, built on the contradictory principles of freedom and slavery, still represents the best hope for mankind on earth.

Early European immigrants came to America in search of a better life, while Africans were brought here in chains as slaves. It stands to reason then, that one's view of America would be predicated, in large part on how he came here in the first place, and the experiences of his forbearers subsequently. Consequently, as an African-American, my conception of this great country is derived from the view of the descendent of the slave.

America's founding document, The Declaration of Independence, holds that "all men are created equal." This phrase places the belief of equality as a founding principle. Yet all people were no treated equal in 1776 when the Declaration of Independence was signed and adopted. The Declaration of Independence goes on to state "that we are endowed by our Creator with certain unalienable rights, that among these are Life, Liberty and the pursuit of Happiness." Again, these noble principles were not extended to all.

This document serves to remind us all, however, that as Americans, we are bound by our common humanity. It challenges us to repel those deeply emotional urges within us and seek higher levels of being. It also serves to remind us that in our own quest for freedom and justice, our hope shines out as a bright beacon of light to all mankind around the world.

History has recorded the enormous physical and emotional abuse associated with the "peculiar" institution of slavery and its long-lasting negative effects on the human spirit of both the slave and the slave master. This legacy was ingrained in our national psyche and even today, remains a challenge to our national unity.

History also records that African-Americans served valiantly in every war and earned the respect and admiration of the whites they served with. About

5,000 African-Americans, both free and slaves, fought for American freedom during the Revolutionary War. They fought and died in every important battle. Thousands of slaves fought in the Union Army soon after the Emancipation Proclamation was written. Approximately 200,000 African Americans fought for the Union Army during the Civil War.

African Americans fought in World War I and World War II in separate units and won medals for their courage in battle. They also served with distinction in Korea and Vietnam.

Notwithstanding their military as well as their extraordinary physical and mental contributions to this nation, racial justice has come slowly in America. It took a Supreme Court decision in 1954, 178 years after the signing of the Declaration of Independence to outlaw segregation in public schools, and civil right legislation of the 1960s to bring about equality in public accommodations.

As an African-American born in 1939 in the south, I lived in a segregated community, attended segregated schools and went to a segregated church. Even after the civil rights legislation of the 1960s, the community is still segregated, the school is still segregated, and the church is still segregated.

I went on to have an outstanding career in the Federal Bureau of Investigation and a second career as a corporate executive. Unlike my own experiences, most of my high school graduating classmates had few opportunities beyond high school. In recent years, opportunities have increased and many more doors have been opened to people of color in recent years. It is said that we are now limited only by our own imagination and diligence.

My own individual triumph and similar successes of other African-Americans is a demonstration of the resilience of the human spirit. African-Americans have succeeded at the highest political and corporate level positions. Right can overcome wrong and truth can prevail. The walls of segregation can crumble and all people can be embraced for their contributions in making this nation great.

Over the centuries, American democracy has improved and gotten stronger. Today, we stand at the beginning of the twenty-first century, and turn a new chapter on the American experience. America is the richest and most powerful nation in the world, yet we are still struggling with our racial divide.

For over 200 years since the signing of the Declaration of Independence, America has made uneven but steady progress in creating a strong democracy. Much has been accomplished, while much remains to be done. We have worked for peace around the world and for fairness and justice at home.

The threat of terrorism and the war against it, challenge not only our national security but our freedoms as well. We must balance the difficult tasks of aggressively pursuing those who would harm us, while maintaining our cherished freedoms that epitomize us as a nation.

With each new national election in America, there is new hope and a look to a brighter future. There is the renewed belief that ingenuity will triumph greed, and that we will overcome our visceral self urges and indeed rise above them.

In the current political season it is interesting to note that of the three leading candidates for the Presidency of the United States, one is a senior citizen, one is a woman and the other is an African-American. This symbolizes the promise of America, no matter who emerges as victorious in November. Anyone can succeed if he or she has a vision of the future and is willing to work hard to accomplish it.

The hope of America is the hope that no matter where you were born, how humble your beginnings, or who your parents are, that you can rise up to the principles embodied in the Declaration of Independence and the Constitution. The greatness of America is in this hope, and it is reborn in every political season and in every major national accomplishment.

What America Means To Me

Erin Connolly
River Vale, New Jersey

Even though I am only thirteen years of age, I have found that America is an amazing nation. The majority of Americans truly believe that this nation is a symbol of freedom. It may be difficult for some people of other nations to understand that here in America I can play and hold hands and be friendly with young girls my age regardless of race, religion or nationality, without fear of being punished. I am so proud of the protection that police officers give to our communities to keep us from getting hurt by some bad people. Police officers and firemen risk their lives every day to keep us safe and healthy and that is exactly what my two uncles do, they are police officers, Uncle Bob and Uncle Chris. I love everything that America represents in addition to freedom, the spirit of the people, the love for our flag, our colorful parades, our pledge of allegiance and especially our national anthem, all of this makes me so proud to say, this is what America means to me.

What America Means To Me

Robert Galantucci
Founding Partner of the Law Firm, Galantucci & Patuto
Hackensack, New Jersey

America, it is more than the beauty of the land – the mountains and streams, the oceans and lakes. It is more than the individual liberties we enjoy, the freedom to be ourselves, to speak and worship as we see fit. It is more than the American Dream to succeed and flourish and pursue our happiness. Mostly, it is the community of a wonderfully diverse people, respectful of all that has been given to us. That is the majesty of the America I know.

What America Means To Me

Chief Robert J. Kugler
Saddle Brook, NJ – Police Department

Simply put, America means the environment of the freedom to choose one's course and destiny for his or her contribution to society. When the word "America" is thought of, there are emblazoned mental symbols that are almost inherent in each of us, including the United States flag, the Star Spangled Banner National Anthem, the motto "In God We Trust" and, most unfortunately, 9/11/2001. America is the Divine Protector of its inhabitants. America provides not only the freedom and protection for society, it allows us citizens to each engage our perseverance in our daily walk in our own way. America provides us with the mind-set that "if you want it bad enough, keep working for it." America reminds us not to dwell in despair, don't keep harping on "I got a raw deal" and blaming it on others. America idolizes integrity and character and holds our hand even in bad times. America is one of the most ethnically diverse societies and facilitates close family life. Prior to the tragedy of September 11, America was a place where historical war type events were almost naturally understood to be part of our life. 9/11 changed that for many. When we heard of our brave armed forces losing their lives fighting for our country, we were deeply saddened but understood to some degree that their losses were a potential life-changing event to happen for many. When the tragedy of 9/11 occurred, the images of innocent people becoming a part of the losses changed all that.

America wants us to love and forgive, not get angry and get even. Not only do we need to love and forgive more, but to learn from the events as well. The saying, "history repeats itself" is only for those who don't listen the first time. America is a land of inhabitants who have varying personalities and visions. America needs more prophets and fewer whiners. America needs the prophets to spread the gospel of respect to one another. America will conquer the evil thought of hatred through these prophets. America will provide for the generations and generations of its people through God, Liberty and Law. May God continue to bless each of us, through us and for us.

What America Means To Me

Dick DeAngelis
President, DeAngelis Management Services, Inc.
Fairfield, Iowa

It means One Nation Under God – not that we have the "exclusive rights" to the Creator, or that we are the only country that acknowledges that God exists. It's just that we recognize that we possess certain inalienable rights which come from the true "Father of our Country," that Primal Source of all Creation who leads us to do great things and challenges us to champion Freedom and Equality for all men and women.

Take a second and imagine, right now, what life would be like if someone had control over you to tell you where you could work, where you could live and even could tell you whether or not you could say a prayer to God. How would you feel if you couldn't leave that situation or give hope to your kids to leave such repression. I believe Americans must continue to fight anyone who wants to take those freedoms away. For it is those very freedoms which allow us to aspire to do great things in this world and achieve our higher purpose.

To America And Freedom:
What America Means To Me

Dr. Bill SooHoo
Chairperson, Professional Security Studies Department
New Jersey City University
Jersey City, New Jersey

It was another summer day in 1960 at the Ho Kheng Laundry on Broadway in the Bushwick section of Brooklyn, New York, which my parents scraped and saved to own. I was helping out in the front when a man came into the laundry and asked to speak to my Dad. It was strange to me because he was a distinguished white male, dressed in a suit and tie, and not someone we were accustomed to seeing at the laundry especially in a neighborhood that was predominantly African-American and Puerto Rican. We were the only Chinese family in the area. I recall telling this man when he asked to speak to my father, that my Dad did not speak English very well. He then asked if someone else was there who could help. I told him my older brother, however he was out, but I proudly proclaimed to him that I also spoke English. He smiled as it must have been obvious to him as he replied, "I'm sure you can young man." At that moment my mother came to the front and asked me who the man was. After telling her that she was looking to speak to Dad, she asked me to find out where he was from. I did and I told Mom that he was from the FBI.

Up to that time, I had never met an FBI agent before, but heard of the them and believed it was some kind of special police type agency—but special. Mom told me to let him in and to help translate until my older brother returned home. I normally would have gotten my Dad myself but for the past month or so he wasn't feeling well and I recall Mom telling us to leave him alone. During that time I do not think he had spoken a single word and seemed very upset, almost sad. The FBI agent proceeded to ask about an air mail letter that he received recently from Communist China about a month ago. When I was translating I remembered that letter because I was accustomed to the blue colored air mail letters – the type that you wrote on, folded and glued that my parents would send to China to their families. But this time, the letter the FBI Agent was referring to was not blue-colored. It was a light brown and the stamp on it was embossed with the head of Mao Zedong, the head of Communist China.

That also struck my memory because I was the one who received that very piece of mail from the postman about a month earlier. When I saw this strange piece of mail I immediately called it to my Mom's attention. She took one look at it and took it immediately to my Dad. Now I remembered. It was shortly after my Dad read the letter that he started to act strangely and Mom told us to leave him alone. Well I got to translate most of the interview for the FBI Agent before my older brother came home and took over. It was then that I realized that the letter was from the Chinese Communist Government and it basically said that my Dad's sister, my aunt, was executed by the Communist Chinese because of her refusal to abide by the Communist way. Later on I found out that my aunt did not leave China with my parents in 1949 when the Communist under Mao Zedong won the civil war. She wanted to stay and work with the Catholic Maryknoll missionaries. It was the first time I had ever seen my Dad cry and that image of him will forever remain in my memory.

After this incident, my parents would from time to time remind me of the evils of communism and what they did to my aunt, and the reasons for why they left their homeland. They came to the United States to start a new life and provide my two brothers and me the best opportunity to succeed. This is not a rare story as many Chinese immigrants of that period left China for the very same reasons. This was not unlike America's first immigrants who came to America to escape religious persecution in the 17th century. My parents were just a continuation of the melting pot that America had become. I believe I was eight years old at that time when this incident happened at my parents' laundry in Brooklyn. It was an auspicious omen of things to come.

Thirty-one years had passed since that time. It is now September, 1992 at Langley, Virginia at the Headquarters of the Central Intelligence Agency (CIA) when it struck me. While walking up the stage to receive an award from the United States Intelligence Community, I glanced over at my mother and father who stood up and clapped with tears in their eyes. It was at that very moment, that all the things I used to take for granted became important. Their long hours at the Ho Kheng Chinese laundry on Broadway in the Bushwick section of Brooklyn, New York, yielded another reward for them. Those years of washing and ironing shirts and linens, were a means to an end. I could see for the first time why they were so proud. They had made it. Not that they ever doubted it, but their decision to leave China after the communist takeover, and come to

America was indeed the right one. Oh how happy I was on that day. I truly realized how fortunate I was that they had made these sacrifices to leave their home, come to a foreign land where they had no roots, did not speak the language, with little else than the clothes on their back so that their children would have a better future, and a better opportunity to be successful.

It was then that I realized that this was not about me, but about what they did and what America had provided them. The land of the free and the home of the brave had given them the opportunity to provide and flourish so that they could experience days such as this. Yes, the American dream did work as they had heard and they watched me, their second-born son receive the National Intelligence Medal of Achievement, the civilian equivalent of the military's Legion of Merit. I was among one of the first FBI Agents to ever receive that award.

It was 1949 shortly after the revolution, when my parents, Yin (Chester) and Chui Woo (Rose) SooHoo left China for Hong Kong to escape communist oppression, not unlike the many Chinese of that time. A year later with nothing but the clothes on their back, they arrived at Angel Island and waited to be processed for entry into the United States of America.

My mother still remembers the day when my father and uncle were initially processed and left for New York City, while she and my aunt waited to be processed in Angel Island. The first thing my father bought for himself and my uncle with the nickel he had in his pocket were two glazed doughnuts. It was a moment he would always remember, his first purchase in America. It was a place where he would begin new roots for the benefit of his family.

I can still remember those Sundays when the entire family would take the subway or occasionally a taxi to Chinatown, and while my brothers and I were studying Chinese, my parents took English lessons so that they could become American citizens. I can still remember how my older brother and I would help them prepare for the interview with Immigration and Naturalization, asking them who the President of the United States, the Governor of New York and our State Senators. And on that day when they were finally naturalized as American citizens, you could not wipe the smile off their faces.

Although my Dad, Yin SooHoo, passed away in June 2005 at age 97, he would live to see his three sons grow and prosper, with his oldest son Joseph becoming a computer systems analyst, his youngest son Lenny, comptroller at a major music company in mid-town Manhattan and me, his middle son, retired as a Special Agent of the FBI at the end of 2002, and began his second career as an Assistant Professor, completing his Ph.D., and is now Chairperson of the newly formed Professional Security Studies Department at New Jersey City University, a new department that has received three national recognitions, and as of this writing will be hearing as to whether or not this department will be designated by the National Security Agency (NSA) as a Center of Academic excellence.

This is what being an American is about. At New Jersey City University, many students are like myself, the first in their generation to live in America. For many of them English is not their first language. Many are also among the first in their families to receive a college education. This is what being an American is about. Coming to America and taking advantage of the opportunities provided to start a new life for themselves and their families. The baton has been passed and I now work with these students with similar backgrounds and stories. Each and every time they succeed, I feel I have given back to the country that will forever make me proud to be an American. It is not something I will ever take for granted.

Every now and then, I will stop at a doughnut store, reach into my pocket and buy two glazed donuts. While having my doughnuts and cup of coffee, I remember the first purchase my Dad made in America, look up to the heavens and smile at my Dad and thank him for the tremendous sacrifices he made for us, and making me a very proud American and son.

What America Means To Me:
America – You Will Only See It When You Believe It

Al Parinello
CEO, Parinello Enterprises, Inc.; Founder, Preserve The American Dream
Old Tappan, New Jersey

Nestled on the Hudson River directly across from New York City, Hoboken, New Jersey, was for decades refuge for thousands who immigrated to America. Such immigrants included my grandparents who believed that, unlike the poverty of their European roots, the streets here were paved with gold. Sinatra aside, it was my home for the first 20 years of life.

I don't know when I first heard it, but I listened and I listened well. My elders gifted me the words that would define my adult life. "Work hard," they told me, and "treat everyone with the same respect you would want from them." This coupled with "play by the rules—play fair" were the concepts that I embodied as a child. And, these words were always followed by the natural conclusion that "This is America, anything is possible here."

I was born into a family that bordered on poverty. My parents fought every day until my mother couldn't take the abuse any longer; she scooped up my three young brothers and me and started the divorce proceedings from a safe haven at a loving aunt's house. We had soup for dinner most of that time, all we could afford. But, I didn't know the difference, because it couldn't possibly matter to the Television Producer in my mind. Television was friendly. That's where my real life was lived, not in those gray, cold-water flat walls.

I looked forward to the assemblies at Joseph F. Brandt Grammar School. The assembly was a place that was not a classroom. It was bigger than life. They were theatrical performances and became my favorite place and the closest place I knew that was like my fantasy life in my mind. The best part was the salute to the flag and the singing of the National Anthem. This gave me hope. It gave me meaning in a world that was, at best, both confusing and depressing. When mine contributed to those hundreds of little voices enthusiastically reaching, ***"And the rockets' red glare, the bombs bursting in air, Gave proof***

through the night that our flag was still there, the thrill was shivering and I became proud at the same time to be part of this great country, and I would defend her from that moment on.

I like to think of my life as the fulfillment of the American Dream. That scraggly boy who had little but an imagination and great gifts from his elders went on to a wonderful and joyous life in television and other forms of media. I'm a published author, I've created national television programs, I've created, produced and hosted a talk radio program syndicated internationally, I've owned and run my own highly-rated radio station and produced over 100 rock concerts and plays, I've executively-produced an independent movie and I'm currently owner of a web development firm and in the development stages of producing a Broadway musical. I don't tell you this to brag. I'm more astounded than you can possibly be. I accomplished these things because I'm an American. Given the same state of beginning circumstances anywhere else in the world, the end results would pale in comparison.

America is a place where virtually anything is possible if the motivation is correct and the desire and willingness is present to work hard and play by the rules. Unfortunately, today, America and the American way of life are being attacked by an enemy that can only be created in the many free liberties given to the people of this great country. The enemy within wants more than it deserves. It wants guarantees. The one necessary and unchanging caveat that comes along in a free society where we can all define our lives in any way we wish is that it does **NOT** come with guarantees. Guarantees are for the lazy and uncommitted. Freedom comes with responsibility and it comes with honor and bravery. It also comes with a helping hand when needed. But, no guarantees. To those who wish to fight for guarantees, I can only ask the most tried and true question:

Oh, say does that Star-Spangled Banner yet wave o'er the land of the free and the home of the brave?

The answer is a resounding YES! Let's keep it that way.

What America Means to Me:
Family Ties
Bound by Love and Patriotism

Chief Frank L. D'Ercole
Former Executive Assistant, Police Bergen County Law and Public Safety
Institute
Norwood, New Jersey

Gustine and Filamen D'Ercole had a son, Francesco D'Ercole, born in Italy on December 18, 1895. They lived in a little town called Chieti located in Abruzzi Province. Italians traditionally think of Abruzzi as a remote mountainous region; its eastern border is marked by vast sandy beaches stretching along the Adriatic north and south of Pescara.

Francesco, my father, decided to migrate to America in 1909. He was just fourteen years old and at his young age traveled on a ship alone to the land of opportunity. He arrived in America and went through Ellis Island like many other immigrants. Francesco came from a humble beginning in Italy and began his quest when he lived with his older sister, Josephine, and her husband, Jack D'Angelo, on a farm in Dumont, New Jersey. He worked on the farm until he was in his early twenties.

Francesco met my mother Carmella, who was born in America on January 29, 1902.

Carmella was seven years younger than Francesco; however, it was love at first sight. They decided to get married in 1925. They opened a vegetable stand around the corner from their family two-bedroom flat on East 102nd Street in New York City. Francesco and Carmella had five children (all girls) with no boys in sight. Italian custom requires that there must be boys to carry on the family name. So, Francesco went to Italy to visit his family and it is said in a family joke that Francesco went back to Italy to get the formula to start having boys. It must be true because our family expanded with the next four children were boys then a girl, a boy, and girl totaling twelve children.

In 1941 Francesco and Carmella were tired of the vegetable stand and with a growing family decided to look for a farm. They found a house in the wilderness of Norwood where townspeople still milked cows and slaughtered their own pigs. The police force had two full-time officers and there were few roads. Most residents still traveled by horse and wagon through often muddy ground—ground that made it impossible to wear a good pair of shoes.

So, Francesco and Carmella purchased the Farm for $5,000 and they along with their nine children moved to the wilderness of Norwood. I was only a year old and the last child born in New York City (three weren't born yet). The farm is located between Rockland Ave. to the south and Northvale Borough line to the north. The area was known as the patch because most Italians lived in the area and the gardens were extremely bountiful.

However, within two years, Carmella's Brother Joe (Uncle Joe) with his wife and brood moved in upstairs. Our dream of having our own room was put on hold because the Grassi family (our cousins) moved in to help pay the cost of the house.

As in most Italian families everyone was named after each other. We had Upstairs Larry, Downstairs Larry, Upstairs Frankie, Downstairs Frankie, Upstairs Joey, Downstairs Joey. If someone called "Joe" both would come running. We played games like kick-the-can and hide-and-seek and had our own baseball games. We grew up with our cousins with a total of 24 children living in the farmhouse that is now a three family house. We used cow flop for our bases. You'd squish into it if you were safe. We were most of the time barefoot because who could afford shoes? We never got athlete's foot.

There were many advantages of having a large family – whenever a kid got whooping cough or chicken pox, all the kids were quarantined. What a way to get out of school.

My brother Gustine and my sister Philomena were named after my grandparents which is the Italian custom. I am named after my father "Frank" and all my other sisters and brothers are named after cousins, aunts, and uncles. The twelve of us have the same godparents, Nicholas and Mary D'Angelo, who owned a farm in Paramus where Bergen Mall now stands.

Francesco was a very hard-working, strict Italian who demanded that all his children work hard at whatever they did. He wore a four-inch wide belt but never had to use it to discipline his children; he would just look at them and put the fear of God in them. The family did not have many material things but had much love and happiness with twelve siblings running around the house. Italian custom usually requires that the oldest son becomes the leader of the family, so it was that my brother Gus became the rule of the roost when my father wasn't around.

The D'Ercole family was generous. To this day people recall that during World War II, soldiers from nearby Camp Shanks came to the farm when food was not plentiful and as with all Carmella D'Ercole customers, people would bring their bags and ask for 10 cents worth of spinach or other vegetables but would leave with a bag filled by my mother. Charlie Amoroso from D&E Uniform always tells me how his parents would send him for 25 cents worth of vegetables and my mother Carmella would fill up his bag and give him back the quarter to spend on himself.

One of the most vivid memories of our youth was when the War ended. We all got on the back of my father's 1936 Federal Farm Truck. My grandmother was banging two pot covers together. We were flying the American flag, and my father driving and blowing the horn as we drove around Norwood. There were three cloth dummies hanging across Rockland Ave.; one of Hitler, one of Mussolini and one of Hirohito. Brother Gus reached up from the truck and punched one of the dummies causing the legs to fall off.

The prior owner of our house was owned by a bootlegger who made applejack in the cellar during Prohibition. The house and barns were filled with tunnels and the D'Ercoles still make wine in the tunnel that leads from the house to the barn.

In the 1952, the D'Ercoles built the first greenhouse and slowly transformed the garden farm into a thriving Garden Center. In the early part of 1960 my father Francesco, the family patriarch, suffered a stroke. The family interest expanded and was not solely in farming and the Garden Center. The D'Ercoles were strongly involved in the community; brother Larry started after serving as a Councilman for nine years and then brother Gus served on Norwood's Board of Adjustment. He served as a Councilman and then served as Mayor for more than twenty years. Brother Joe had farming in his blood and followed in our fathers footsteps. Brother John left the farm to a career handling real estate for the United States Post Office. We have a special bond because we share the same birthday, November 15, but he was born in 1938 and I was born in 1940. John always says that the best birthday present he ever got was when he was two years old when I was born on his second birthday.

My whole family stood by my parents (especially my sisters) during the many years they were sick an eventually passed on. Sister Lucy predeceased my parents and sisters Phyllis and Joann passed away after my parents. Our other sisters Adeline, Marie, Anna, and Carol still are connected to the farm.

Sixty-seven years later, every one of our nieces and nephews, great-nieces and nephews all live in Norwood and Northvale.

As in the case of the entire D'Ercole family since arriving in Norwood in 1941, we never left farming. However, on October 15, 1964, I was appointed as a patrolman on the Norwood Police Department. I rose through the ranks being appointed in 1967 to Sergeant an in 1969 to Lieutenant, and to position of Police Chief in 1973 – a position I treasured and held for over thirty-two years. Law Enforcement got under my skin and at 65 and still going, I landed a position as Executive Assistant for Police at the Bergen County Law and Public Safety Institute. My career took me on a wonderful journey where I met so many great people and friends.

I have been blessed in many ways; my wonderful family, my lovely wife Maureen, my children, Colleen and her husband Matt, Brian and his wife Christine, Kristen and her future husband Christopher and my Irish grandchildren Matthew, Caitlin, Ryan McGowan and my Italian Grandchildren Frankie and Victoria D'Ercole.

I am honored to be part of the Bergen County Police Chiefs Association, one of the greatest police organizations that anyone could belong to. I was honored to serve the association in every position and honored to be President of the association in 1984.

In 2003, the Rockland County Columbus Association, sponsor of the Columbus Day Parade announced that my brother Gus, Joe and I were chosen to be Grand Marshals. It was one of the many best days of my life. I was such a proud Italian-American marching in the Columbus Day Parade in Pearl River.

I don't know where I am headed on this wonderful journey, but I leave my destiny in the Lord's hands. God Bless America, my family and friends.

What America Means to Me

John Birkner, Jr.
Mayor of Westwood, New Jersey

I recently had the honor of walking behind the Westwood Fire Department Color Guard in a parade. What I noticed most about that experience were the spectators along the parade route. People of all ages lined the streets, but it was what only small percentage did that struck me, and caused me to ask myself the question, "What does my flag mean to me?"

Along that parade route I saw patriots, mostly from our "Greatest Generation" stand and salute when our flag approached and remain standing until it had passed by. Many clearly needed assistance to get up from their seats, some were unsteady on their feet, and in one case a man with his Army cap rose from a wheel chair. Now please understand, I am not saying that those who did not get up were unpatriotic. What I am saying is how many times have we ever really thought about our flag and its meaning? All too often we may take it for granted since we see it everywhere as it is displayed all around us on everything from soda cans to store windows and advertisements, we may not ask ourselves that question, "What does my flag mean to me?" Our greatest generation knows what it means and in their own subtle way they never stop teaching us, or reminding us just what the American flag symbolizes.

It symbolizes what the thirteen colonies were founded on. It symbolizes a nation once divided, now united. It was proudly flown on those Flanders Fields, the beaches at Normandy and in the South Pacific. It symbolizes the cause in Korea, Cambodia, and Viet Nam. Our flag rose from the rubble at the World Trade Center, the Pentagon, and in the farmlands of Pennsylvania when some sought to destroy it. Now our flag brings hope to the mountains of Afghanistan, and the desserts of the Middle East.

Every color means Liberty, every star means Liberty, every stripe, every thread, and every fiber means Liberty. Our flag reminds me every day just, "What America Means To Me."

Chapter Thirty Five

The Rebirth of Patriotism

By: Albert F. Chestone

Over the years almost every community in this land we love, has heard the blaring of trumpets, the timely beating of drums, the distant sound of a bugle echoing "taps" that grips our hearts causing our eyes to overflow with tears as we silently recall those individuals, who made the supreme sacrifices for us, so that we might enjoy our Freedom, and our Democracy. We take pride in our many colorful parades to celebrate some historical event that relates to the richness of America. We are proud of the many ethnic parades held through-out this land to celebrate cultural customs, for which All Americans support because such parades further strengthens our patriotism for America.

Accordingly, I am prompted to ask you the reader, now that you have taken some of your leisure moments to read this book that contained heart-felt patriotic reflections, including expressions of gratitude and concerns of notable authors regarding America, do you feel a bit more patriotic and moved to do all that you can to keep America Free and Safe from those among us, who aim to destroy "Our America" from within? Hopefully, all of us will forever thank God for the honor and privilege of being Americans, and to be ever mindful of how fortunate we are to have been born in this Great Country or to have had the honor and privilege to be naturalized as an American.

Yet, in spite of this great honor to be an American, it is so difficult to comprehend why there are "Anti-Americans" in our midst, who have nothing better to do, than to take advantage of their right to "freedom of speech" in order to find fault with anything and everything about our form of government. They definitely fit in the mould of "rabble-rousers", who enjoy stirring the "pot" that over-flows with anger for the sake of anger, in order to destroy our "pillars of patriotism, and our pillars of strength" because they lack Faith, Hope and Charity. They prefer to wage an uncivilized battle in order to claim victory for Satan, by removing God from our thoughts, our practices, as well as from any and all references to Him on our coins, currency or buildings that bear inscriptions that glorify Him.

TO WHOM CAN WE TURN FOR ACTION:

It only seems proper to challenge our Federal Legislators, by simply asking if they are willing to step forward and take action to effectively curb and prevent these constantly growing movements by various bands of Anti-Americans, to cease once and for all, in their efforts to "re-write" our treasured governing historical documents by renouncing God in deference to the beliefs of Our Founding Fathers, as well as the beliefs of the Christians, who are in the majority in America. Can We Americans, The Patriotic Judaic/Christians and Patriotic People of other faiths depend on most of our Loyal and Proud American legislators, to take immediate and effective action to protect "with enforceable laws" the honorable practices, and customs including all references to God, to continue, be it in our Pledge of Allegiance, Our National Anthem, coins, currency and inscriptions on our various government or public institutions, now and forever?

As we continue to place Our Trust in God, we shall pray that most of our legislators will also embrace this SACRED TRUST IN GOD, as did Our Founding Fathers.

THE BIBLE HAS NO SUBSTITUTE BOOK?

Through-out our rich history, whenever an individual is privileged to be selected, elected and accepted, to assume the responsibilities as a government official, he or she takes the proper oath of office, as all loyal Americans have done since the early days of our history, by placing his or her left hand upon a BIBLE AND NO OTHER SUBSTITUTE BOOK and raises his or her right hand as a patriotic sign of belief and allegiance to America. There should be no exceptions to this practice. Can we count on one or more strong patriotic federal legislators to step forward and introduce SUCH LEGISLATION?

THE POWER OF JUDGES AND THE SUPREME COURT OF AMERICA:

The dictionary defines in part that a "Judge is a public officer, who is invested with authority to determine litigated questions". Further "a Judge also has the power of arriving at a wise decision, based on discretion and discernment". Most, if not all Americans respect the office and responsibilities of Judges. The duties of a judge are obviously different let alone stressful regardless of the level of the court of assignment.

Having established this fact, I am particularly interested in the authority and rulings of the Supreme Court of the United States of America consisting of learned men and women. This Court is the highest judicial body in the United States Government. We are aware that the men and women chosen to this high judicial body are brilliant, honorable and dedicated servants to enforce laws that will best serve to protect citizens of America.

Mindful of this premise, I am moved to request this loyal group of American Judges, to search their hearts and souls, as did Our Founding Fathers, and proudly and unanimously write a binding Declaration that adopts the religious acceptance OF GOD BY AMERICA, so that the Anti-God Americans among us, will no longer in their "minority status", attempt to persuade the courts, to remove God from our coins, and currency nor the references to Him in the form of inscriptions on our buildings, or from religious TV and Radio broadcasts, including Prayers in Schools, Prayers in Sporting Events, or public displays of Crèches, Menorahs, etc. . . . . IT IS TIME THAT THE JUDAIC/CHRISTIAN, SILENT MAJORITY BE GRANTED A LONG OVER-DUE FAVORABLE DECISION REALIZING THAT IT IS "IN GOD WE TRUST", a belief embraced by our Founding Fathers. "Our silence as Christians, has been tempered, because of our civilized humanity, based on our firm belief and convictions in One God, The Father Almighty. However, now is the time for one or more real strong Judaic/Christian believers among our legislators, to clearly state and document the safeguards of the religious beliefs and practices, of the Judaic/Christian Majority of Americans, which are historically etched in the decisions of our Founding Fathers, all of whom had placed their Trust in God. This being said, "radicals" are free to continue to embrace the teachings of Satan, but they are not free to destroy our religious beliefs nor "Mock Our Risen Christ".

THE UNITED STATES OF AMERICA IS PREDOMINANTLY CHRISTIAN:

It is well known and officially documented that the United States of America is predominantly a Judaic/Christian Nation and certainly as such, respects both, "the believers as well as the non-believers regarding the existence of God. We are a nation, that is tolerant of All Religions and Beliefs. However,

America does not and will not accept nor embrace religions or so called religious groups" that adhere to the teachings through verbal instructions or written material in any format, advocating the killing of "human beings" or for the planned destruction of particular nations. Therefore, let it be known that any "radicals" of any religion, who advocate death and destruction should not under any circumstances or guises, attempt to practice nor spread their beliefs within the borders of these United States of America, because "WE THE PEOPLE:, WE THE JUDAIC/CHRISTIANS, as well as all other peace loving religious faiths, will resist any and all such possible attempts. AMEN

SOME PATRIOTIC REFLECTIONS ABOUT "A WHY AND A WAY".

It is my hope, that this patriotic book has served some purpose in assisting you to be a little more informed about the Greatness of America and why we feel the way we do.

- Why we feel so thankful when we see veterans marching in a parade, or children walking to school, or people coming out of church.
- Why we get a lump in our throat whenever we hear our National Anthem.
- Why we feel like standing and applauding, too, when Congress rises as one at State of the Union Address to greet our President.
- Why we believe in Patriotism, Respect, Decency, Morality and Honesty.
- Why we respect Our Flag, Our National Anthem and Our Pledge of Allegiance.
- Why we are proud of Our Form of Government, Our Humanity and Our Heritage.
- Why we are proud of Our Own English Language.
- Why as a Judaic/Christian Nation, we Place Our Trust in God.

Now I ask all of you to join me in the rebirth of patriotism in America. I am hopeful that, "What America Means To Me", will help the momentum last forever. I know that most if not all, who read this book, have been justifiably rewarded by the patriotic writings and expressions that were set forth. It is further desired, that some of you will be inspired, perhaps to become future leaders of our Great Country. Most importantly, it is my wish, that this book, even if in a small way, has filled you with some additional pride, knowing that you are an American and truly aware of the importance of Freedom, Patriotism, Faith, Hope and Charity. May we as Americans continue to grow and strengthen our Patriotism, Maintain Our Faith in God, Hopeful that America will always remain Strong and that we will always be a Kind, Compassionate and a Charitable Nation, so that when tragedy strikes anywhere on this planet, America will continue to be the First Responders. Yes, this is America, and This Is What America Means To All Of Us, because we "Pledge Allegiance to the Untied States of America and to the Republic For which it Stands, One Nation, Under God, Indivisible, with Liberty and Justice for All". Amen.

We the Patriotic Americans, We the Patriotic Judaic/Christian Believers, We The Patriotic Believers of Other Faiths, must remain united in our efforts to make certain that all elected officials on all levels of government in addition to those, who represent us within our Federal Government, MUST by their words, deeds and actions provide all the safeguards to keep America strong as One Nation Under God in Whom We Trust. We The People must be constantly assured that all elected individuals, who serve on various levels of government, be held accountable to his or her oaths of office, and in the ethical execution of their particular governing responsibilities.

Chapter Thirty-Six

Patriotism Is Our Source of Strength

By: Albert F. Chestone

I am hopeful that having read this book, you will have been somewhat inspired to continue your journey as proud and patriotic Americans. To be all that you can possibly be as an American and to convey why you feel as you do about this land you love, America.

Our actions and expressions of patriotism will unquestionably touch the hearts and minds of our young people whether native-born or new to our country, so that they will also capture strong and lasting feelings of patriotism, thereby providing the basis for them, that they might better grow in knowledge and wisdom to better serve their country and their God.

It seems so difficult to comprehend why over the past several years there appears to be a planned movement by individuals, organizations as well as some radical groups to undo what our Founding Fathers had created, to make America a lasting democracy, with the firm conviction that it was the hand of God that blessed this land and planted the seeds of freedom for mankind.

Yet in spite of all the freedoms that everyone is entitled to and enjoys in this great nation, there are those among us, who seek to do all in their power, to take advantage of their God-given freedom to deny and strip this Judeo/Christian Nation of its practices, handed down by our Founders and subsequent Presidents as it relates to our flag, our Pledge of Allegiance, our coins, our paper money, our humanity, our heritage and to most things that loyal patriots treasure—our freedom.

Perhaps the many beautifully written chapters contained in this book by outstanding brilliant authors might be the spark needed to ignite the minds of rabble-rousers in America to stop their efforts in attempting to destroy the very fabric of America, by simply understanding, that America has become a great nation based on the sacrifices and dedication of the early settlers and our Founding Fathers.

The questions that remain for those who wish to destroy us by removing God from our practices and beliefs, are as follows: How did America manage to survive since the early days of the pilgrims' arrival seeking religious freedom? How was it possible for America to survive since the signing of the Declaration of Independence in 1776 by Christian founders?

How has America managed to survive thus far as one nation under God? What harm, what catastrophic developments have occurred, as a result of the dedicated athletes, young boys and girls of grammar school age, young high school and college men and women, as well as our proud young men and women engaged in professional sports, who form huddles for prayer and unity prior to a sporting event? What earth-shaking harm has been caused by proud Americans for singing our National Anthem or God Bless America, whether in the great assembly halls of our government institutions or in a high school or university assembly hall, or at particular sporting events? So I ask, is it because of this patriotism, that the world will end in fire? Is there a fear that there will be mass conversions to Christianity? Will all sporting arenas collapse and cause chaos if the National Anthem were to be sung and the Pledge of Allegiance recited? Who will be offended, especially when you consider that over 85% of Americans are of the Judeo/Christian belief?

Are those of us of this faith supposed to cave in and abandon all that has been given to us by our Founding Fathers and the Lord, based on a concocted fear that we might offend, perhaps a certain few? What contagious diseases will grip all humans in America if the inscription, "In God We Trust" is reflected on our coins and paper money or references to Him are inscribed on outer and inner walls of public or government buildings? What deadly plague will claim the lives of all Americans if a creche, a manger, a menorah or any God-adoring symbol is reverentially displayed on private or public grounds? How can God-loving people experience strangulation and ultimate death by a cheerful and joyful exchange either in writing or vocally, during the Christmas season with the comforting words: Merry Christmas, Happy Hanukkah and Happy Kwanzaa. We live harmoniously with all peace loving individuals regardless of their religious beliefs.

I also invite your attention to the words of a former great President of our nation, Theodore Roosevelt:

> The true Christian is the true citizen lofty of purpose, resolute in endeavor, ready for a hero's deeds, but never looking down on his task because it is cast in the day of small things, scornful of baseness, awake to his own duties as well as to his rights, following the higher law with reverence, and in this world doing all that in his power lies, so that when death comes he may feel that mankind, is the same degree better because he lived.

For those who seek to destroy this country from within, you might wish to heed the words of Theodore Roosevelt. In spite of your God-given right to enjoy the freedom of speech, let us however be mindful that while you have the right and privilege to speak and write freely in a civilized and respectful manner, you do not have the right to say and do things that are detrimental towards the best interests and security of the United States of America.

All patriotic Americans believe in America and are convinced that patriotism is our source of strength.

We are a nation of law and order and we Pledge Allegiance to the flag of the United States of America. We salute all patriotic Americans, especially those in the military service, and we shall always be mindful of their contributions, including the many of whom have died, so that we might continue to enjoy our freedom and our form of government.

We proudly acknowledge with great respect the protection afforded us night and day by so many honorable and dedicated individuals in the field of law enforcement on a federal, state and local level. We take great pride in our respective police, sheriffs, and state troopers, including our brave and courageous fire fighters. We salute all patriotic Americans, our entire work force, the infirmed, those who assume household responsibilities, all those engaged in the medical and legal professions, our teachers, professors, and students, all those, who render a service for the well-being of America.

We are confident that our young people realize that in order to live in a free society, they must prepare themselves mentally and morally if they are to assume the role as future leaders whether in politics or within their respective communities.

I am hopeful that this book will serve as a basis for renewed inspiration to uphold the love and respect for our flag, our National Anthem, our Pledge of Allegiance, our form of government, our humanity, our heritage, our own English language, and to be ever mindful that we are a Judeo/Christian nation under God.

America is definitely the land where impossible dreams can come true, provided an individual assumes the total responsibility to improve and increase his or her knowledge, in order to contribute to society in a meaningful manner, and thereby enjoy a certain standard of personal living.

Anyone and everyone can dream about attaining the American dream, but dreams can only be realized if there is a combination of serious effort and determination. America is without question a land of opportunity that allows one to dream dreams that are reachable. Dreams are beautiful to experience, but one must be awakened to the reality that in America, through hard work and determination, impossible dreams can come true. Therefore, we as patriotic Americans are believers in the spirit of America and prepared to defend ourselves against those who seek to destroy America from within. We shall remain strong, and never will we surrender to the anti-Americans among us nor to any radical extremist religious groups seeking to dominate the world.

Lastly, it is quite evident that there are some people in certain countries throughout the world who have openly expressed their dislike and hatred for America. This of course is their right, but it is unfortunate when you consider the fact that all peoples of the world are aware that America is by far the most responsive, caring, and generous nation in the world. It is also sad to think that some nations that were about to sink and perhaps vanish from the face of the earth have been vocal in their hatred for America, forgetting that it was "America's Life-Line" that saved them from the depths of despair. Perhaps this is the moment, the time, and the hour, when peoples of all nations of the world might wish to seriously read and comprehend, a message that bespeaks volumes about America, who we are and what we are about.

The following is a genuine expression of gratitude for America, which was credited to the former Prime Minister of England, Tony Blair, in a statement to Parliament: "The only people outside of Great Britain to shed their blood for England, was the American soldier and Jesus Christ."

Lastly as the author, I am confident that all the patriotic Americans who have read this book will continue on their patriotic journey and crusade for the good of America. Let us insist that our patriotic legislators and judges on all levels of government take appropriate and meaningful action to prevent the spread of unwanted, unacceptable, anti-American political cancer once and for all. The time is now for our government officials to show their true patriotic colors and beliefs by preventing this political cancer from spreading, and to begin restoring the teachings and examples of the courageous men and women, whom we read about from another era, and known to us as the founders of our country. It is time to reach back into our rich history and re-learn the process involved to re-strengthen our great nation.

America's alarm clock has rung – it's time for America to wake up before we are slowly dominated by some slow moving but shrewd evil force. Perhaps it's time to ask our legislators and judges what he or she has done or is doing to make and keep America strong not only in matters dealing with patriotism, employment opportunities and prosperity, but in preventing the spread of the anti-American political cancer here and abroad. Many years ago, a man named Norman Thomas, who was a presidential candidate on six occasions for the Socialist Party of America stated: "The American people will never knowingly accept socialism, but under the name of liberalism they will adopt every fragment of the socialist program until one day America will be a socialist nation without knowing how it happened." Mr. Thomas died December 19, 1968.

As a Judeo-Christian Nation, we must NEVER surrender our Democratic way of life nor our Capitalistic system by falling prey to a Socialistic form of government.

We should never forget an important equation in which our great nation is anchored:

Democracy + Capitalism=Freedom +Prosperity.

Let's get America moving and booming again. In God we trust. Amen.

About the Author

Albert F. Chestone, born and raised in Waterbury, Ct. Earned his BS Degree Ohio University, Athens, Ohio and Masters Degree, New York University. Veteran WWII Air Force, Africa /Italy. First wife, Marcie, graduated OU, died 1980. Had 5 children of this union. Al served almost 30 years with the FBI. Currently married to, former widow Lorraine Ryan. Founder of the Westwood Swim Club, Westwood, NJ; 1st President, Pascack Valley Crime Stoppers; Past Chairman, Pascack Valley DARE Program; Past Chairman, FBI, Northern New Jersey (Bergen County) Chapter; Past President, St. Andrew's Parish Council, Westwood; One of the Founder's of St. Andrews Church 50 Plus Club; Assisted in initial development of the former Pascack Valley Hospital, Westwood. Member, Phi Delta Theta Fraternity; Bergen County Police Chief's Association; The American Society for Industrial Security, (ASIS); Society of Former FBI Agents. Past President, Supreme Associates, Recruiters of Security Directors for Corporations. Currently involved in programs dealing with Water Conservation. Author of two books, "My Parting Gift" a guide for families before a crises strikes and "What America Means To Me".
E-Mail: AChestone@optonline.net
Website: http://www.wamtm.com

LaVergne, TN USA
06 January 2010
169137LV00002B/11/P